£2.95

THE PONY CLUB

The Pony Club was founded in 1929 and now has about 43,000 members in Great Britain with a further 80,000 overseas. If you are not already a member and would like to join, please write to The Secretary, The Pony Club, British Equestrian Centre, Stoneleigh, Kenilworth, Warwickshire CV8 2LR, enclosing a stamped addressed envelope. You will then be sent details of your nearest branch.

edited by Toni Webber

Copyright © MCMLXXXIII by The Pony Club.
All rights reserved throughout the world.
Published in Great Britain by
World International Publishing Limited.
A Pentos Company,
P.O. Box 111, Great Ducie Street, Manchester M60 3BL
Printed in Belgium.
SBN 7235 6690 9.

Contents

You and Your Pony

The Pony Club, with its worldwide membership, has been teaching and encouraging young riders for more than 50 years. Now they have produced a new video series of teaching programmes for young riders entitled **You and Your Pony**. From simple advice on how to mount and dismount correctly to more advanced teaching in dressage and gymnastic jumping, this series is designed to improve the knowledge and skills of the rider in easy stages. Although primarily aimed at young riders the cassettes provide a useful reference for riders of any age.

Pony Club

Annual

PONY CLUB PONIES

**photographs by
Sally Ann Thompson
Bob Langrish
Mike Roberts**

Welsh
Pony

"My pony's Welsh." How often has someone said that to you when you have asked her what sort of pony she has? Sometimes, riders are more honest. "Oh, I don't know. Probably Welsh." The truth is that Welsh is used to describe almost any sort of cross-bred pony standing between 11.2 and 13.3 hands high, especially if it is a good sort of pony which winters well, jumps reasonably willingly and is prepared to put up with most gymkhana hazards.

Most of these unregistered ponies do indeed have some Welsh blood in them somewhere, but they could just as easily have Dartmoor, Exmoor, Shetland or New Forest blood. The reason that most people pick Welsh to describe their ponies' ancestry is that it is one of the most popular of all the native British breeds. Study the breed classes at any show – the biggest are always the ones for Section A Welsh Mountain ponies and their slightly larger cousins, the Section B Welsh pony.

This is not really surprising. Welsh Mountain ponies are very pretty. Their dished faces, little, leaf-like ears and handsome tail carriage are legacies from their Arab forbears. They are small

New
Forest
Pony

Shetland
Pony

enough for children to handle and care for, yet big enough to cope with most Pony Club activities. A very large number of them are grey – and grey is a colour which many people like best. So even if they don't know for sure what type of pony they have, riders generally plump for Welsh.

A good Pony Club pony like this one should enjoy jumping as much as its rider does.

Exmoor Pony

Thirty years ago, Pony Club activities were limited to working rallies, fun rallies and a few inter-branch competitions for older members. Today, competitions are regularly organised for everyone, right down to the youngest children. Minimus jumping, mini one-day events, even dressage contests, are available for the smallest members.

The most useful Pony Club pony, therefore, needs to be an all-rounder, capable of jumping both show and cross-country jumps, able to take part in mounted games, amenable to the discipline of dressage, safe in traffic and with other ponies and hardy enough to live out all the year round.

Pony Club camp teaches children to look after their ponies entirely themselves. A young rider may be perfectly able to cope with a large, well-schooled pony when she is on its back, but if she cannot reach its head in order to groom it properly or has difficulty placing the saddle on its back, then many of the lessons learned at camp will be wasted on her.

One of the most important

criteria, when picking a Pony Club pony, is to match the pony to the child. The British Isles have such a wealth of different pony breeds to choose from that this should not be as difficult as it sounds.

The smallest pony breed is the Shetland, and a good Shetland will give a young child a wonderful start to her riding career. Unfortunately, not all Shetlands are good. Far too many of them have a will of

A three-year-old on a Shetland pony – under supervision.

their own and, because they are strong and obstinate, they like to take charge.

Small legs bashing away at the saddle flap make no more impression on the pony than a fly. Small hands tugging at the reins will not stop a determined pony from heading for the nearest patch of lush grass. And their enchantingly pretty faces begging so sweetly for a titbit can quickly turn into a scowl and a set of sharp teeth if the pony doesn't get what it wants.

Many people consider that a Shetland is too broad in the back for young children, but this seems a minor drawback if his temperament is kind and tractable.

A really nice child's pony and one which is particularly suitable as a first pony is the Dartmoor. This hardy little pony from Devon, with its neat, attractive head, strong, compact body and fine, free action, makes a perfect schoolmaster. By nature, it is so kind and sensible that it can be trusted to build up a young rider's confidence through the early years of riding activities.

If you have set your heart on a grey, there is no alternative among small ponies to the ubiquitous Welsh. And indeed you could go a long way and do a lot worse than settle for a Section A Welsh if you want a small pony or a Section B pony for a bigger child. One advantage of Welsh ponies is that they hold their value, and opportunities for showing them in hand or in ridden Mountain & Moorland classes are widely available.

Dales Pony

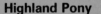

Highland Pony

Fell Pony

They are capable of all Pony Club activities and the best of them are very adaptable, suiting their behaviour to the ability of their riders. The same pony can be gentle and careful with beginners yet lively and active with more ambitious children.

For a strong, willing pony, capable of surviving on minimal

Connemara Pony

keep and ready to tackle anything, the Exmoor is well worth considering. The oldest breed in Britain, it is descended from the Celtic ponies of prehistoric times. Its native habitat, the wild, high moorland of Devon and Somerset, has made it naturally shy and alert. An Exmoor needs careful handling but, properly broken, it is a first class Pony Club pony, well able to carry out any work it is asked to do.

The Exmoor is distinctive in appearance. Bay, brown or mouse-coloured, it is characterised by prominent eyes ('toad' eyes) and a mealy muzzle. The creamy colour of the muzzle often extends to its belly and inside thighs.

For Pony Club members at the height of their interest in ponies and riding, the New Forest pony is an ideal mount. These ponies range in size from 12.2 to 14.2 h.h. and are categorised by the New Forest Pony Breeding and Cattle Society into two definite types. Type A, up to 13.2 h.h., is a light-boned riding pony with all the best characteristics of the breed — courage, intelligence, docility and willingness. Type B is similar, but bigger, suitable for the young adult or teenager.

Both types of pony are quick to learn and can be schooled to act sensibly and bravely both inside and outside the ring. They make excellent hunters, are impervious to traffic and respond easily to people.

For a jumping pony, the best breed is the Connemara from western Ireland. The true Connemara is a wiry pony, standing no higher than 13.2, but the breed has had a strong infusion of Arab and Thoroughbred blood and bigger ponies of 14 to 14.2 are now common. Indeed, on lush pastures it has a tendency to grow even bigger.

A Connemara or Connemara-cross is an excellent mount for older Pony Club members and associates, especially if they are keen to make show-jumping and horse trials teams. Temperamentally it is intelligent and kind, physically it is strong and deep-girthed, with the sloping hindquarters that denote jumping ability.

The former pack ponies of northern England and Scotland — Dales and Fell ponies and Highland ponies — have been rediscovered as riding ponies in the last thirty years. The smallest of these is the Fell pony

which usually stands between 13 and 14 hands high. It is a very muscular pony, with a thick mane and tail and some feather. It seems to have unlimited stamina, especially at the trot, and is perfectly capable of undertaking any Pony Club activity.

Its bigger cousin, the Dales pony, is probably more suited to the adult rider looking for a sensible mount for hacking and long distance riding, which, because of its hardiness, is easier to keep than a horse. The Dales is a powerful, muscular pony, with a luxurious mane and tail and plenty of feather. With its strength and stamina, it is used more for pony-trekking than for Pony Club work.

There are two types of Highland pony. The Western Isles version is more suitable for children than the bigger Mainland, or Garron, variety. Both are naturally docile but slightly wary of strangers. Well-broken, however, they are honest and hard-working and extremely sure-footed. The Western Isles pony is much used by Pony Club members for all manner of activities, although the Garron, which averages 14.2 h.h., is more popular for trekking work.

With so much indigenous material to choose from, it is no wonder that riding in the British Isles starts at a young age. Visit any Pony Club camp or working rally and you will see a wide variety of ponies represented, in most cases ideally suited to their riders' different temperaments and riding ability.

The efforts of various breed societies and the compulsory licensing of stallions have, in recent years, almost banished the coarse, rough, nondescript 'mongrels' of the past, and even ponies without a formal pedigree now display many of the best characteristics of the British native breeds.

CHILDREN on HORSEBACK

Riding styles and clothing change from generation to generation. But the pleasure children get from their ponies never alters and nor do the ponies themselves.

Children must have been riding horses for as long as there have been horses tame enough to ride – that is, close on 4,000 years. But we have no idea how much effort was made in ancient times to teach children to handle horses.

The earliest book on horsemanship in existence is *The Art of Horsemanship,* by the Greek writer Xenophon, who was a cavalry officer and published the work in about 360 BC. He wrote it for grown-ups, but there must have been plenty of aspiring young riders who followed its advice.

After that, we know very little. By the Middle Ages, most grand households had resident riding masters and the sons of the house – and sometimes the daughters – attended riding lessons regularly.

In the 16th and 17th centuries, the emphasis rested on the ideas of the great classical riding masters from the Continent. Little boys spent many a long session in an indoor riding school learning High School movements.

As fox-hunting developed in England in the early 18th century and more and more of the countryside was enclosed, the ability to ride boldly across hedges and ditches came to be regarded as the greatest accomplishment. This must have given child-riders a wonderful feeling of freedom. However, we can still only guess at the way children rode. Most of the portraits of children on horseback were painted to please their mothers, and were not very true to life. Look, for instance, at the early prints on these pages.

The little boy lounging so nonchalantly on his grey pony would probably have lasted on its back no more than a few seconds if he had really chosen to sit like that at a meet. And what about Colonel James Grant, painted at the age of five by the Victorian artist, William Salter? What a pretty little boy and how proud his fond Mamma must have been of him! But more unsuitable clothes for riding in would be hard to find. And if I had been young James's mother, I don't think I would have trusted the gleam in his pony's eye.

A much more accurate representation of a boy on his pony is the painting by Sir Edwin Landseer. You can just see that little boy buzzing around the countryside looking for fallen logs to jump. And his position in the saddle is entirely natural.

Once the camera was invented, records of children on horseback become easier to find. They are interesting in particular because they illustrate the way that riding styles have altered and pinpoint the differences in the ponies' tack and the riders' clothes that have come about over the

Portrait of a boy on his pony by Sir Edwin Landseer (1802–1873).

years. At the same time, they show how little the ponies themselves have changed.

Take the picture of Margie on Captain, photographed in 1870, for example. Margie is dressed in a serviceable but voluminous riding habit – the skirt covering her legs completely – and a smart little velvet hat with a curling feather. Her pony looks a nice schoolmaster type. He would probably go well in a snaffle although he is having to put up with a long-shanked curb.

On to the first part of the 20th

century. Look at the contrasting styles in the two photographs of girls on horseback. Honor Story and Joan Cluff were pictured on their ponies in 1907. They are wearing skirts over leggings and their jackets are heavily puffed at the shoulders (this was the era of leg o' mutton sleeves) but their hats, unusually, are velvet-covered hard hats very similar to today's, and they are riding astride. Joan and Monica Sheriff, on the other hand, are side-saddle, and only Joan on the left has a skirt to her riding habit. Monica is dressed in breeches and leggings in spite of the side saddle, which seems an odd way to dress when attending a meet of the Duke of Rutland's Hounds. The ponies' manes are hogged – this was a common practice with riding horses until well after the Second World War.

Meet of Foxhounds – John Leech, a Victorian artist (1817–1864).

The Young Cavalier, portrait of Colonel James Grant, then aged 5, by William Salter (1804–1875).

Miss Honor Story and Miss Joan Cluff, 1907.

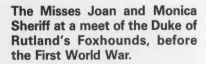 Margie on Captain, from a sepia photograph taken in 1870.

The Misses Joan and Monica Sheriff at a meet of the Duke of Rutland's Foxhounds, before the First World War.

Riding at shows produced a variety of dress. The boy on the rather thin-necked, long-legged pony, posing with his parents, Sir Gilbert and Lady Greenall, and his younger brother, was photographed after winning a rosette at the International Horse Show, Olympia, in 1911. His cap is the kind that boys habitually wore in those days, both on and off their ponies. The way he sits in the saddle is typical of the style of riding which was taught right up to the 1950s before the development of the modern, deep-seated saddle encouraged the rider to sit well down in the middle of the saddle and before riders were taught to get their lower legs further back.

Joyce Purvis on Mousie was photographed after winning reserve prize in the children's riding competition at the Bath Show later the same year. Like the other children, she has her legs well forward, and her outfit was no doubt considered extremely smart, with its long-skirted coat and matching leggings. Her hat, however, looks modern, an indication that some horsemen recognised the importance of protective headgear. It seems odd to see her pony without a noseband, especially as she has come straight from the show ring, but you will notice that ponies in some of the other pictures are without nosebands.

In the years between the wars, school hats were very much the order of the day. Miss Liddell, seen with her friend Miss Grant, at a meet of the Ludlow Foxhounds in 1923, seems to be in her school skirt, stockings and school coat as well. However, the extra rein on the snaffle bit suggests that she is only a beginner, perhaps at her first Meet, so possibly her parents had not yet bought her a proper outfit.

Children were never considered too young to learn to ride, and basket saddles were popular for the very young. Little Barbara Renton, aged 21 months, claimed to be the world's youngest jumper when she was photographed on her pony, Cuthbert, being led over an obstacle by her mother at the newly-opened National School of Equitation at Roehampton Vale in 1927.

A very popular form of hat was the soft, velvet jockey cap worn by 4½-year-old Susan Scarfe at the opening meet of the Garth Hunt in 1938. Of course, older children, like Bill

Dewing, aged eight, preferred a bowler – it was easier to doff, and good manners are always important.

The spectacular leap by a young rider was made at a horse show in Billingshurst, Sussex, in 1939. The horse is Blue Sky, the rider Master E. Hicks. Master Hicks wears his school cap and blazer although it is clearly quite a big show.

I find the photograph interesting for two further reasons. One is the fact that Blue Sky has two martingales – a running one and a very tight standing martingale. He also has a single-rein Pelham bit with what appears to be a jointed, twisted mouthpiece, quite a severe bit for a juvenile jumper.

The other interesting feature of the picture is the obstacle the pair are jumping. It demonstrates very clearly the flimsiness of show jumps in those days. Although it is a big jump – a double oxer, in fact – there is no form of in-fill at all, and it must have been quite

difficult for a horse or pony to judge its take-off correctly. You can also see laths resting on the poles. These were commonly used for competitions judged under B.S.J.A. rules. If a lath fell, the competitor was penalised half a fault – there could be no rapping of the pole and leaving it intact as happens these days. A horse either cleared the fence cleanly or it lost marks. The rules differentiated, too, between front and hind-leg knock-downs – the first incurred four penalties, the second, two.

Finally, yet another jumper, this time taking the Road Closed fence in the Junior jumping at the National Pony Society's show at Roehampton in April 1947. Today, this young boy has fulfilled the promise he displayed over 35 years ago and is one of our best known and best loved show jumping personalities. Can you put a name to him? If you are really stuck, turn to page 60 for the answer.

If you are really stuck, turn to page 60 for the answer.

One of today's best-known show jumpers competing in the junior jumping, April, 1947.

ROAD CLOSED

WHAT A DAY TO GO HUNTING

Whatever the weather, nothing causes so much enthusiasm as the Pony Club meet

by Antoinette Russell

THERE HAD been gale warnings all morning and the view from the window showed that they were entirely justified. The trees in the garden were bent almost double and a fine wetting rain spattered the window panes.

"Are you sure you want to go?" I asked my eleven-year-old daughter doubtfully as I straightened her Pony Club tie. She gave me a withering look.

"Minnie would be just as happy in his nice warm stable," I added, thinking what the rain would do to the brand-new riding hat, not to mention Minnie's spankingly clean tack.

"It's the Pony Club *meet*," Charlotte said. *"Everybody's* going."

"Well, they might change their minds," I said weakly, but Charlotte was already out of the house, the bridle over her arm.

Fifteen minutes later, Charlotte and her friend, Rebecca, were setting off on the twenty-minute hack to the meet. Both ponies were as clean as any grass-kept pony can be in the middle of winter; both had been stabled for the night to allow the mud to dry, both had had every vestige of surface mud removed, although a little cloud of dust rose if you patted them. Their long manes had been coaxed and twisted into stubby plaits (an hour's effort, these) and their hooves shone with oil.

They're both mad, I thought, making preparations to follow them to the meet in the car. Nobody will be there.

But I was wrong. Nearly seventy children were milling round the forecourt of the Five Bells when I reached our local inn. I recognised many of them from rallies and gymkhanas earlier in the year but rarely have I seen them looking so smart, in spite of the weather. Their ponies ranged from shaggy Shetlands to elegant small hunters, which shivered slightly as the wind whipped round their full clips and the rain clamped their pulled tails tight against their quarters.

A fair sprinkling of adult riders was out, pressed into service to act as nannies to those children who were hunting for the first time. Some

of the smaller children looked doubtful about the whole enterprise; the old hands stood in groups, chatting together as they waited for the huntsman to arrive with hounds.

It was a foul day to be hunting, but the children's meet comes but once a year and huntsman and whippers-in were determined to put a brave face on it.

"Any foxes about?" asked the huntsman of the gamekeeper's son, who was attending the meet on foot.

"Plenty, but I warrant you won't find any today."

"Oh well," said the huntsman, "we can but try."

The field moved off to the

first covert, Charlotte and Rebecca keeping well to the rear. It was Rebecca's first time out – Charlotte hunted twice last season but Minnie, her new pony, was an unknown quantity.

"Is he all right?" I asked anxiously.

"Of course he is. Don't *worry!*"

Before hounds were put into the first covert, the children were given a short lecture on hunting, its methods and manners. Normally, this talk is quite detailed, with time allowed for questions and answers, but today, with the wind whipping the Master's words away, it was doubtful whether any but the children nearest to him actually heard what he was saying. He kept his lecture short, and left it to the Field Master to shepherd the children to the far side of the covert, well out of harm's way.

The countryside here is mainly pasture and woodland, with the fields divided by hedges and a fair amount of wire. The landowner is a keen supporter of the hunt and hosts the children's meet every year, giving orders that all hang gates should have their top rails removed and all possible jumping places made easy for the children to negotiate.

I made my way on foot across three fields, ducking my head against the driving rain. In the lee of a small copse I found other parents and together we scanned the rising ground ahead with its stand of woodland on the top. It was hard to pick out one's own daughter among the blurred figures in front of the trees.

We watched them for a while as they moved back and forth from one covert to another, and presently, thinking they were heading away from us, we left the shelter of the copse and cut across the fields, hoping to see them have better luck further on. But then they doubled back yet again and I was close enough to ask Charlotte how Minnie was going.

"Fine, fine," she said casually. "Except that the reins are so wet that my hands keep slipping and I can't hold him." However, she seemed to be holding him well enough and I watched her negotiate in reasonable style a small Sussex gate. Rebecca on Bowsy had one stop, but he is only 11.3 and the ground was very boggy so his lapse could be forgiven. There were plenty of bigger ponies which had to suffer the ignominy of having the gate taken down.

One of the 'nannies' came up to us foot-followers. "Could anyone here take charge of Polly? She's had enough." A generous parent offered to take Polly and pony home in his trailer — and that was one problem quickly solved.

Soon afterwards, I decided that, like Polly, I too had had enough. Back home, I prepared Minnie's box and set a bran mash to 'cook' under a hessian sack. I expected Charlotte back in an hour or so, but it was well after 3.30 before I heard hooves outside the kitchen door and went out to find child and pony muddied to the eyebrows but ecstatically happy.

Later, with Minnie munching hay contentedly in his box (he spurned his bran mash — perhaps I didn't make it very well), and Charlotte, pink, shiny and clean after a hot bath, I asked about the day.

Oh, it was wonderful, wonderful! Bit by bit, the details emerged. No, they hadn't seen a fox; yes, Minnie jumped very well; yes, he pulled a bit; well, they'd spent a lot of time standing around; yes, it was *frightfully* muddy, and oh, glory, she'd never get the tack clean again, but everything was wonderful.

I had time to reflect that this, really, was what the Pony Club was all about. In those distant days before the war, more than half-a-century ago, this was what Brigadier General Tom Marchant and Major Harry Faudel-Phillips had founded the Pony Club for — to introduce the younger generation to the joys of hunting and to ensure that hunting would continue.

Today, the Pony Club is the nursery for riders in so many disciplines that we tend to forget that the safeguard of hunting was the organisation's original aim. Although the majority of the branches still bear the name of the hunt in whose country they were formed, there are many areas which have no parent hunt at all. Other branches have split and re-split as membership has grown, and at the other end of the line some packs have merged and now hunt over an area two or three times larger than it once was.

These packs often find themselves linked to three or four Pony Club branches. Where this is the case, the hunt usually tries to fit in a children's meet for each branch.

At a Pony Club meet, the cap is normally reduced to Pony Club members, although they will be expected to pay a full cap should they wish to hunt on other days. For any newcomer to the hunting field, the children's meet is the perfect place to learn what hunting is all about, from the etiquette of hunting and the countryside to the jobs performed by the various hunt officials. As with any sport, you will find that your enjoyment is heightened when you have a deeper understanding of the skills involved.

Some hunts invite older members of the Pony Club to act as whippers-in or as Field Master on a children's day. Some Pony Club branches try to get their members together *before* the meet — in a village hall, say, or even at the hunt kennels — where hunting can be explained with few distractions. Much depends on the individual Master and the degree of co-operation between the District Commissioner of the branch and the parent hunt.

But few can deny the enthusiasm which exists among Pony Club members for any opportunity to go hunting — my daughter's experiences last Christmas holidays bore witness to that. How many more children might have attended the meet had the weather been better? The future of hunting today is threatened by greater forces than existed fifty years ago and it has become more important than ever to foster a proper understanding of hunting and the countryside. The Pony Club meet is one of the best ways of doing this.

Getting your Pony FIT for Camp

by Peter B. Clarke B.V.Sc., M.R.C.V.S.

Most Pony Club camps last for about a week. During that time, a pony is working four to five hours a day and, when he is not actually being ridden, he is confined to a loose box or to his place on the horse lines.

For the average pony, out at grass and accustomed to being ridden at weekends and occasionally after school, camp brings both a complete change of routine and an alteration to his diet. It is neither fair to the pony nor safe to expect him to be able to cope without any preparation at all.

A pony is a herbivore, which means that he normally lives on grass. If you intend to change his situation by taking him off grass, feeding him hay and concentrates and keeping him indoors, even if it is only for a week, it is vitally important to introduce the changes gradually. If you don't, your pony could get colic. A very severe attack might be fatal.

So when you rush to mark the dates of Pony Club camp on your calendar, turn the pages back five or six weeks and write START GETTING MY PONY FIT FOR CAMP.

Five or six weeks are just about sufficient time to acclimatise your pony to living indoors and eating extra food. During that period, you should slowly increase his daily food and exercise.

To begin with, work out what concentrates your pony will need at camp. The amount will depend on what size and type of pony you have. If you are not sure, ask one of your Pony Club instructors. Hard feeds are usually given night and morning, although some ponies require a small feed at midday as well. In the weeks beforehand, start by giving small quantities and gradually increase the feeds until you have reached the right amount.

Work out a schedule of exercise, too, starting slowly and building up to a programme of two hours' work a day. Some flat work will be helpful to both of you, but vary the work by taking the pony out for a ride and walking and jogging along lanes. It is important to see that your pony does not get bored.

If you can, start bringing the pony into a stable either overnight or for a few hours each day. As most Pony Club camps take place in the summer holidays, your pony will benefit by being brought in during the afternoon and early evening, when biting insects are at their most annoying.

If it is not possible to stable your pony at all, you can still prepare him for camp by following the regular feeding and exercise programme.

Ponies must be well-shod for camp, so this is another date for your calendar – BOOK THE BLACKSMITH. Remember that lots of other Pony Club members will be trying to get the farrier at the same time, so be sure to ring early. It is best to have your pony shod at least a week in advance to give the new shoes time to settle down.

Where camp is taking place at a racecourse, every pony must have a valid anti-'flu vaccination certificate. This is to comply with Jockey Club regulations, but the protection is just as important at *any* Pony Club camp. The initial doses must be given between 20 and 90 days apart, followed thereafter by regular, annual booster doses. A pony has to be rested for up to 14 days following the injection so don't wait until the last minute before getting your pony done.

By following these quite simple rules, you will arrive at camp with a fit, healthy pony, able to take part in all the activities, who will enjoy the week ahead as much as you.

GOING CAMPING

photographs by James Hackett

A racecourse is the perfect place to hold a Pony Club camp. The members' bar and the jockeys' changing rooms make ideal dormitories and loose boxes built for racehorses offer five-star accommodation for small ponies.

Every summer holidays, the Southdown Hunt East branch takes over Plumpton Racecourse, a National Hunt course tucked under the South Downs. It's a week of hard work and a lot of fun — as these pictures show. They were taken by James Hackett, whose daughter is a Southdown East member. He spends the whole week at camp, in charge of stables, but every so often sneaks out with his camera to record the goings-on.

Everything except bedding has to be brought to camp by each member. First morning at the entrance to the stable yard sees a flurry of parents and older brothers and sisters humping hay bales and food bins.

Vet's inspection. Every pony has to be inspected by the vet to check that it is fit enough for camp. This is the moment most dreaded by each camp member. Every year one or two ponies fail the test, but usually alternative mounts can be found.

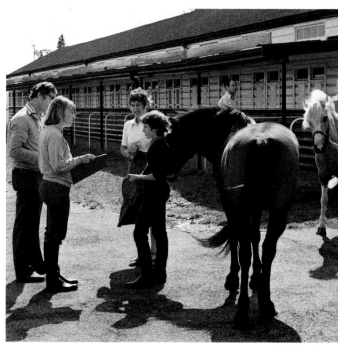

Settling in.
Each pony is allocated
one of the racecourse
looseboxes . . .

... from which he can watch with interest everything that is happening.

Notices are pinned up in the stable yard. A new arrival anxiously scans the lists to see which ride and team she is in.

Mucking out. For some members, whose ponies are normally kept at grass, this is the first time they have had to practise stable management.

Tack-cleaning is a chore which is best carried out in company. In wet weather a group settles down under cover in an empty loosebox.

But it's more fun to clean your tack outside when the sun is shining.

And there's always time for a shared joke.

Saddling up for a ride. Members are divided into groups according to the standards they have reached and the size of pony they are riding.

Leaving the stable yard. Instruction takes place in the centre of the oval-shaped racecourse.

Checking the sitting position, with stirrups crossed in front.

Exercises help to improve balance. A rider practises the 'scissors' movement, while the others look on, knowing that it is their turn next.

A rider negotiates the makeshift jumping lane.

Camp is not all ponies and instruction. A neighbouring swimming pool has been borrowed for some off-duty relaxation.

In the members' bar, in the evening, a few of the riders gather together to discuss the events of the day.

Mealtime. Members queue up for a lunchtime salad. Food is provided by mothers and catering supervised by voluntary helpers.

Instructors and supervisors pause for welcome refreshment.

Memento of camp. The group photograph is a traditional feature.

Last day is Parents' Day and Prizegiving. Every member receives a camp rosette and a team rosette, and individual points awards are made as well. The District Commissioner gives away the prizes.

Camp is over for another year. The racecourse reverts to normal. Last goodbyes have been said and members promise to be back again next year.

PUZZLE PAGE

HORSE'S HEAD CROSSWORD

Clues Across

3. Class for the youngest riders (7,4)
8. Grecian vessel (3)
9. Horseshoes are made of this (4)
12. What you did to your pony before entering 13 across (7)
13. Part of the showground (4)
14. The spine forms a bony this (5)
15. Cockney horse (3)
17. Cut and laid obstacle (5)
20. British Show Pony Society (abbr) (1,1,1,1)
22. You can't ride this horse (3)
23. Third eyelid (3)
24. Soft saddle (3)
25. Royal Artillery (abbr) (1,1)
26. About (2)
27. Worn by a jockey (6,4)
28. Type of horse for toddlers (5)
29. Horse colour (3)
30. Scottish negative (3)
31. Dad (2)
32. This is put on the roads in winter (4)
36. Horse dealer (5)
39. What a pony did to his food (3)
41. Say this firmly when your pony misbehaves (2)
43. Mineral from which metal is extracted (3)
44. Standing or running, it helps to control a pony (10)
46. A show pony should be a good this (5)
48. Avoid blacksmiths who carry out this practice (7)
52. Royal Academy (abbr) (1,1)
54. Aides to Royalty (9)
55. Command when jumping (2)
58. Type of racing horses found on pigs! (8)
60. Foot rest (7)
62. Ponies like more than one for supper! (3)
63. Well worth joining, especially with Pony in front (4)
64. Indian coin (4)
65. That is (abbr) (1,1)
66. Old man or Order of Merit (abbr) (1,1)
67. The Pony Club version has stripes of purple, blue and gold (3)
68. Top of a pony's head (4)
69. Fruity horse colour (10,4)
74. Natural aid (3)

76. Type of horseshoe (8)
77. Negative (2)
78. The goal of a Pony Club mounted games team (7)
79. Straw, peat or shavings (7)
80. Just the rosette we all like best (3)
81. Hang-up for headpieces (6,4)
84. Clumsy person (4)
87. Show ponies point it (3)
88. Type of rug (6,5)

Clues Down

1. Over poetically (3)
2. Gathered horses together (6)
3. Special rein used for schooling (5)
4. Thoroughbred/Middle Eastern cross (5-4)
5. Metal parts of stirrups (5)
6. It's fun to enter this at a show (8,5)
7. Useful for a pony wintering out (3,7,3)
9. Type of cross-country jump (5,4)
10. What you probably like to do to your pony (4)
11. Place in Essex (5)

24

Check your answers on page 60

16. Description of a dipped back (4)
18. Rim (4)
19. Your thighs should do this to the saddle (4)
20. Useful in the stable (5)
21. Jockeys ride with their leathers very this (5)
24. Coloured horse (5)
28. Female of him (3)
33. Cord or twine (4)
34. Coloured part of 75 down (4)
35. Number of faults for a first refusal in the show jumping phase of a one-day-event (3)
37. Horse with some Thoroughbred blood (8)
38. Part of the lower leg (7)
39. 1st person singular of the verb 'to be' (2)
40. A bad-tempered horse may be called this (5)
42. Belonging to us (3)
45. To make this in show-jumping could incur penalties (5)
47. To do with horses (6)
49. Small fish (6)
50. Seabird (4)
51. Home for a horse (5,3)
53. In the Middle Ages the weight of this required horses to be strong and heavy (6)
56. This sort of horse is tiring to ride (6)
57. The only bit allowed in the Pony Club Mounted Games Championship (7)
58. Hunting cry (5,2)
59. Sweet itch may cause a pony to rub himself this (3)
60. Knight's title (3)
61. Writing implement (3)
63. Mane or curry (4)
70. Long distance ride (4)
71. Increase (3)
72. Large bird of prey (5)
73. Young man (5)
75. A good type of pony has a kind this (3)
82. Pronoun (2)
83. Act (2)
85. Either . . . (2)
86. You and me (2)

WORDSEARCH

The following words are all hidden in the letter grid below. They may run up or down, sideways in both directions or diagonally. Can you find them all?

ARCH
BANDAGE
BOOT
BRIDLE
BROWBAND
BUCKLE
CANE
CAVESSON
CRUPPER
CURB

CURB CHAIN
CURRY
DANDY BRUSH
DR BRISTOL
FORGE
GRAKLE
GRASS REINS
GIRTHS
HAYNET
HEADCOLLAR

HEADPIECE
JODHPURS
JOINTED SNAFFLE
KEEPER
LASH
LEATHERS
LIPSTRAP
MANE COMB
NAIL
NEW ZEALAND RUG

PAD
PANEL
PELHAM
POMMEL
PORT
REINS
ROLLER
SADDLE
SHOE
SIDEREINS

SKIRT
STIRRUP
STUD BILLET
SURCINGLE
THROATLASH
TREADS
TREE
WEYMOUTH
WHIP
YARD

S	N	I	E	R	S	S	A	R	G	W	X	S	D	A	E	R	T
M	T	P	U	R	R	I	T	S	R	J	O	D	H	P	U	R	S
J	O	I	N	T	E	D	S	N	A	F	F	L	E	O	T	V	D
I	O	R	E	P	E	E	K	S	K	I	R	T	A	Y	E	Z	N
L	B	L	W	S	P	R	R	A	L	L	O	C	D	A	E	H	A
T	H	O	Z	H	N	E	B	E	E	R	E	P	P	U	R	C	B
E	T	T	E	T	K	I	L	O	G	D	N	I	I	E	T	R	W
L	U	S	A	R	F	N	E	H	S	A	L	H	E	L	H	A	O
L	O	I	L	I	P	S	T	R	A	P	D	W	C	K	R	X	R
I	M	R	A	G	E	G	R	O	F	M	A	N	E	C	O	M	B
B	Y	B	N	L	E	A	T	H	E	R	S	N	A	U	A	Z	R
D	E	R	D	A	N	D	Y	B	R	U	S	H	E	B	T	E	I
U	W	D	R	A	A	T	R	O	P	O	M	M	E	L	L	L	D
T	A	R	U	U	C	U	R	B	C	H	A	I	N	L	A	I	L
S	M	A	G	O	C	A	V	E	S	S	O	N	O	U	S	A	E
H	A	Y	N	E	T	E	L	G	N	I	C	R	U	S	H	N	P

WINNING STREAK

by Cynthia Muir

photographs by
Mike Roberts and
Bob Langrish

Rain marred the first day of the 1982 Pony Club Championships at Stoneleigh, the Peugeot Dressage Championship. Fortunately, conditions had improved a little when the six finalists rode off for the individual title.

Only ten marks divided the first three teams but the Pendle Forest and Craven's score of 414 put them four points ahead of the Beaufort A. Their team consisted of Alison Walters, aged 17, riding Wilton Supreme, her brother David, 19, on Indigo, and Mandy Turner, 20, on Spy Trap.

Their trainer is Mrs Shirley Hindle and the same team should have competed the previous year, but then Mandy's horse went lame and David suffered concussion after a fall, so this result was a splendid compensation for their previous disappointment. The team also received the award for the best team riding their own ponies. Mandy, who is trained by her sisters, helps Mrs Hindle with the training; her Spy Trap is an 11-year-old grey.

"I teach the Walters and many others all through the year," said Mrs Hindle. "All our team regularly attend camp and working rallies and everyone works very hard. We train two or three times a week before the Area Trial and start serious training in June; but, of course, many riders are taking O or A levels which makes things difficult for them.

"The branch stages four dressage competitions, with a cup, one at Christmas, one at Easter and two in the summer holidays, which helps to stimulate interest in this particular discipline."

Alison's Wilton Supreme is an 11-year-old and David's 10-year-old Indigo is an Irish-bred eventer. Indigo must

have felt that Stoneleigh was his second home, for he had a very busy time there. Three days earlier, 15-year-old Sarah Walters rode him as a member of the team which won the Riding Clubs Junior Dressage with Jumping Championship. He was third with David in *his* section, fifth in a section when Sarah rode him in the Horse Trials Championship two days later, and he was also David's mount in the Tetrathlon.

Nicola Sparrow, aged 16, of the Royal Artillery (SP), won the individual Section A, riding Kanzler, from Amanda Taylor, 20, Wylye Valley, on Jehol. The Section B winner was Claire Ballantyne, 15, of the North Staffordshire, on Lochinvar, from Annabelle May, 15, Chiddingfold Farmers, on Coppa Captain. Section C was won by Virginia Strawson, 19, an extremely experienced event rider, with Minsmore, followed by the Beaufort A's 20-year-old Nicola Roden on Baker Street.

SHOW JUMPING

Competitions in the following day's Townsend Thoresen Blue Riband Show Jumping Championship were blessed with sunshine and excellent going. The teams made a brave sight as they paraded, the prize for the best turned-out team going to the Cotswold Vale Farmers, with Mid-Antrim as runners-up. Choice must have been difficult as the standard of turn-out was very high, as indeed it was over all three days – and of the riding, too.

Alan Ball's excellent, not-too-testing course produced twelve teams with no penalties at the end of the first round and four clears each by the Cotley, Ashford Valley, East Lothian and Cleveland. There was a very good performance by one of the youngest teams ever to take part in this competition – the Vale of Aylesbury on their three 13.2 h.h. ponies and one 13.3 h.h. They were Susie Carlsson, Claire Brazil, Nicola Bradley (all aged 12) and Jane Allum, 11.

The course for the second round asked many more

questions. The water was included and the last two fences were a treble and a parallel. After this, just the Ashford Valley and the West Warwickshire could claim a zero score, and they jumped off, Ashford Valley finishing with a winning total of four against the West Warwickshire's twelve.

Mr Draper is the winning team's trainer, and its members were Mandy Whitcombe, 17, on La Rochelle; Maria Draper, 17, on Casual Affair; Sarah Gladders, 15, Norton Flamboyant; and Julie Draper, 19, Wichita Lineman. Mr Draper has a riding and livery stable, the family are most interested in show jumping and his daughters were in the team, so his appointment as trainer was extremely apposite.

"The first year I took over the team, they qualified for Hickstead," he recollected. "And to our delight they were ninth at Stoneleigh. Each succeeding year they have won the Area Trials, and we all have a lot of fun there, staying in the same place each time. This year they won very convincingly.

"We've been so lucky, having good ponies and horses available, and everyone works together extremely well, with a splendid team feeling – to

produce that is what I regard as my chief job. Everyone has to feel that they are all in it together, with no blame to be apportioned to anyone if things go wrong. I am always grateful that my children have had the opportunity to do this and they all learn to take winning or losing as it comes."

Sally Tate on Norgwill Orangeman.

HORSE TRIALS

For the final day's competition, the Domecq and Sunday Telegraph Horse Trials Championship, the weather was very kind, and Philip Herbert's cross-country course of twenty fences, seven of which had 'L' alternative routes, and Jeremy Houghton-Brown's show jumping course proved to have just the right degree of difficulty. Only four teams were eliminated.

Of the cross-country fences, it is usually the Sunken Road which gives the most trouble, and so it proved this time. A good number of faults or eliminations were also incurred at the Trakhener, the Coffin, the Sunday Telegraph Bank and the fence out of the delightfully named Hare's Parlour – zigzag rails over a ditch.

Cheshire Hunt North were in the lead after the dressage, with their score of 128, and the Beaufort, whose dressage tests were ridden late in the day, were eventually their closest challengers, finishing on 137.5. One of the Cheshire Hunt North's riders was unlucky to have a fall on the flat, but all four were clear jumping across country and two incurred five penalties each in the show jumping, so their final total was 138, and this brought them the winners' cup. Beaufort were second with 159½ and Holderness's 186 put them into third place.

In the Junior Individual Championship, Section A was won by 15-year-old Jessica Adkin, Beaufort, on the skewbald Prairie Wind. Christopher Walker, 16, Cheshire Hunt North, on Taskmaster, and Sarah

Kelland, 15, Grove, on Spindle Top, shared first in Section B. Nicola Furness, 17, Berwickshire, won Section C with Barmaid, and the Section D winner was 17-year-old Sally Tate, Hurworth, riding Norgwill Orangeman. Best boys in the respective sections were Steven Chambers, 15, Haydock Park, with Capachino, Christopher Walker, Paul Mingo, 14, East Devon, Cosa Nostra, and Paul's 16-year-old brother, Mark, with Pickles.

There was also a tie for the Greatheart Cup, awarded for the best senior dressage performance, between Ashford Valley's Graham Palmer, aged 20, on Crimdon St George, and Sarah Jenkinson, 18, VWH, riding The Cobbler. Prairie Wind won the Virginian Cup for the best cross-country round by a pony not exceeding 15 h.h.

Juliet Snelson, 20, Wheatland, was the Senior Individual Champion with her 11-year-old mare, Touchwood, a 15.2 h.h. by Fleche Bleu out of a Welsh cob. Juliet is trained by Gillian Watson and she had particular cause for rejoicing because Touchwood had been out of action for 18 months and was making her first competitive appearance since her illness. The result in this competition could not have been closer, for only half a mark separated Juliet from the

Yvette Holland on Coeshall Dawn.

Cheshire Hunt North : Linda Budenbore, Yvette Holland, Rebecca Weston and Christopher Walker.

second, Gail Hancock, 18, Tiverton, on Little Hector.

The Cheshire Hunt North, who were also the best team on their own ponies, were represented by Rebecca Weston, 16, on the 17-year-old, 15 h.h. Brer Fox, a very experienced and successful performer in all fields; Yvette Holland, 17, with the 9-year-old Cogshall Dawn; Linda Budenberg, 16, and her big grey, Fly-by-Night, a 7-year-old by St Elmo; and Christopher Walker on Taskmaster, 11. Both Taskmaster and Brer Fox are by Thoroughbreds out of Connemara mares.

The team all help each other to train, and Linda is taught by Vera Holden, while Rebecca, Yvette and Christopher are trained by Joyce Benson. All compete in BHS horse trials.

"We usually have about ten riders and horses to choose from," Mrs McKenna, the District Commissioner, said. "We send them to as many events as possible to give them plenty of experience, then select the team on their form in these competitions. This year, they won all but one of those in which they took part."

Their performance was a pleasure to watch.

Youngest team with manager Pat Carlsson (Nee Moss).

TETRATHLON

In the Pony Club Tetrathlon Championships, it was good to see the girls' section so well supported, considering that until recently they were not allowed to take part.

The Boys Team Championship was won by Staff College and Sandhurst (Simon and Timothy Hazlem, Michael Woodward and Robin May) with a total of 11,761 points. Nineteen-year-old Robin took the individual associates title with 4260 points. West Lancs County (David O'Brien, Hereward Hughes, Jonathan Curtoys and Gregg Whittington), with 11,598 points, were runners-up. David, aged 17, was second to Robin in the associates title. The best member was 16-year-old Brian Dixon of New Forest (4136 points), and James Evan Cook, also 16, of West Kent Meopham, was second.

Alison Hollington, 17, of Essex Farmers, scored a magnificent 4440 points to take the girls associates title and help her team to victory in the team championships. Her fellow members were Nicola Brett, Joanne Barber and Pippa Hollington and together they scored 12,276 points. Essex Farmers beat Cottesmore (11,812 points), two of whose members, Joanne Cooper, 14, and Susan Wright, 15, finished first and second respectively in the individual members section. Elizabeth Hand of Cumberland Farmers North was associate runner-up to Alison Hollington.

POLO

Polo is still the least widely supported of all the Pony Club Championships, but many of the branches which do take part manage to field more than one team. The Quorn Boxers won Division I of the Handley Cross Cup and Old Surrey & Burstow won Division II. In the Rendell Cup, the winners were V.W.H. who also took the Pardey Cup for being the best team on their own ponies.

In the Gannon Trophy, the Quorn Barracudas emerged the winners, and the Rendell Rose Bowl for the best branch team in the Gannon Trophy Tournament went to yet another Quorn entry – the Quorn Sharks. The Best Turned-out Team award in the Handley Cross Cup Tournament went to Staff College & Sandhurst. Individual awards to riders showing the most promise were made to Grenville Waddington and Victoria Grace.

PRINCE PHILIP CUP MOUNTED GAMES

Seonaid McMillan, forced to drop out of her team the previous year when she broke a leg just two weeks before the championships, made up for her disappointment by helping Eglinton to victory in the Prince Philip Cup mounted games championships at Wembley. This Scottish branch, which trains on the beach when the ground is too hard or too soggy for normal practices, has sent a team to the Horse of the Year Show every year since 1978. They won the cup on that occasion. This year, they also won the Butlin Cup and the stable prize. The team consisted of 14-year-old Seonaid on Olly; Marion Murdoch, 14, Truffles; Robert Murdoch, 13, Fergus; Robert Smith, 14, Ringo; and Craig Mitchell, 13, Trigger.

Blackmoor & Sparkford Vale made a determined effort to break down the lead which Eglinton had established early on. After the first game of the final night, they were only 1½ points away, but a mistake in the next game gave the advantage back to Eglinton. In the end Blackmore Vale (Deborah Trim, 15, Brown Ale; Sharon Adams, 14, Kipp; Janine Scrivens, 14, Hoy; Tessa Dare, 14, Little Mo; and Lisa Antonello, 13, Dusty) finished second.

THE
PONY CLUB

(Incorporated in the British Horse Society)

WHAT IT IS

The Pony Club is a recognised youth organisation for those interested in ponies and riding.

It is represented in no less than 25 countries and has a membership exceeding 75,000.

It is the largest association of riders in the world.

It is a constituent member of the Standing Conference of National Voluntary Youth Organisations of England and Wales.

ITS OBJECT is to 'encourage young people to ride and to learn to enjoy all kinds of sport connected with horses and riding. To provide instruction in riding and horsemastership and to instil in members the proper care of their animals. To promote the highest ideals of sportsmanship, citizenship and loyalty, thereby cultivating strength of character and self-discipline.'

ITS MEMBERSHIP is open to anyone under 21 years of age. Ordinary Members consist of boys and girls who have not attained the age of 17 years. Associate Members are those over 17 years. Membership terminates on attaining 21 years.

ITS ORGANISATION. The unit is the Pony Club Branch. There are 340 Branches in the United Kingdom alone. The country is divided into districts corresponding as far as possible with the Hunts, each Branch being called after the name of the Hunt with which it is connected, e.g. 'The Zetland Hunt Branch of the Pony Club'. Branches may also be formed in non-hunting areas.

Branches are self-contained, self-governing and self-supporting. They are administered by a voluntary District Commissioner assisted by a Branch Local Committee.

The Headquarters of the Pony Club are at the British Equestrian Centre, Stoneleigh, Kenilworth, Warwickshire, CV8 2LR, where the affairs of the Club are managed by the Pony Club Council, which in turn is subject to the control and the direction of The British Horse Society.

WHAT IT DOES

THE WORKING RALLY is the backbone of the movement. Working Rallies are arranged by District Commissioners as and when required, but usually they take place only during school holiday periods. At every Rally some instruction in equitation, care of saddlery or management of the pony is given, combined with mounted games and sports. Dismounted Rallies are also held.

Every member is required to support the Working Rallies of the Branch joined. Failure to do so may lead to termination of Membership.

OTHER FIXTURES include lectures, film shows, visits to kennels, stud farms or other places of interest, horse shows, hunter trials, special children's meets of hounds, summer camps, mounted expeditions and visits of teams abroad.

INTER-BRANCH EVENTS to encourage team work and promote pride in the Branch are another popular feature of the work of the Pony Club and these include a Horse Trials Championship, a Mounted Games Championship (Prince Philip Cup), a Polo Tournament, a Tetrathlon Championship and a Show Jumping Championship.

EFFICIENCY CERTIFICATES are awarded by The Pony Club as an encouragement to members to take an interest in their work and to improve their knowledge. There are six standards of efficiency: 'A', 'H', 'B', 'C+', 'C' and 'D' of which 'A' is the highest and 'D' the lowest. Every member is expected to try for these certificates.

COURSES, including Scholarship courses, are held to train and assist instructors at all levels.

CONFERENCES provide for the interchange of ideas and improvement of methods for all concerned with the running of the club.

INSURANCE. Members and Associates of the Pony Club are automatically insured against Third Party Legal Liability, up to £250,000, arising from their equestrian activities.

WHAT YOU NEED

RIDING CLOTHES. The Rules of the Pony Club require that members shall wear a reinforced riding hat or cap for head protection when attending fixtures mounted, preferably one with a deep crown that bears the 'kite' mark of the British Standards Institution.

The hat should fit the head firmly but comfortably. If it is at all loose and is likely to come off in the event of the rider having a fall, it should be secured by a chinstrap.

The usual dress is a riding jacket and jodhpurs with leather shoes or jodhpur boots, or breeches and either leather or rubber riding boots, a suitable shirt and the official Pony Club tie. In the interests of safety, wellington boots or plimsolls should not be worn.

New clothing is not expected, but what is worn must be clean, neat and tidy.

THE MEMBER'S BADGE. This is supplied by the Branch and should be worn at rallies, shows, when hunting and on all occasions when members meet together.

THE ASSOCIATE'S BADGE. On reaching the age of 17, a member may exchange his/her Member's Badge for an Associate's Badge.

THE MEMBER'S TIE. This tie in the Pony Club colours (purple, pale blue and gold) may be worn by all duly enrolled members.

THE ASSOCIATE'S TIE. This tie is dark blue with embroidered Pony Club Badges, and may be worn by Associates and Officials.

PONIES. Possession of a pony is desirable but not essential. Although the Pony Club cannot itself provide ponies for members to ride, many members hire from riding schools in the district to enable them to take part in mounted fixtures.

The following *are not allowed* to be ridden at Pony Club rallies or events:

Ponies that are very young, or are infirm through old age; ponies that are ill, thin or lame; ponies that are a danger to their riders or to other members or their ponies.

SADDLERY. Saddlery must fit the pony and be in good repair. A 'Pony Club approved saddle' sold at a reasonable price is obtainable from most saddlers. It has been designed to assist young riders in adopting a correct position in the saddle, and to help parents in spending wisely.

'THE MANUAL OF HORSEMANSHIP' is the Pony Club's own book about riding and the care of horses and ponies, and about the care and fitting of saddlery. There are also many other Pony Club publications which will be of help to you.

Note – the officials of the Pony Club are always glad to help you or your parents with advice on any of the foregoing subjects.

HOW TO JOIN

Members join the Pony Club through one of the Branches, normally that nearest home. If you do not know which Branch to join, or do not know the address to which you should send the application, write to The Secretary, The Pony Club, British Equestrian Centre, Stoneleigh, Kenilworth, Warwickshire, CV8 2LR, stating where you live and where you normally ride. Please send a stamped addressed envelope for reply.

Members may belong to one Branch only, but membership of any Branch of the Pony Club constitutes membership of the Club as a whole.

ENTRANCE FEE. The entrance fee is 50p. The entrance fee is payable to the Branch joined.

ANNUAL SUBSCRIPTION. This is £7 (or a maximum of £16 for any one family) and is payable to the Branch joined.

COMPETITION RESULTS

The answers to the 1983 Competition were as follows:

PARTS OF THE PONY

1. Withers   2. White Line   3. Chin groove
4. Bars 5. Dock 6. Pastern

A HORSE FOR NOVICE DRESSAGE

(judged by Lt.-Col. W. S. P. Lithgow, Executive Officer of the Pony Club)

1.   C – A quiet temperament
2.   F – Correct schooling
3.   D – Good action
4.   A – Good conformation
5.   E – Previous dressage experience
6.   B – Strong quarters

The results were as follows:

Seniors (aged 13 to 16)

Winner: Clair Johnson (14), 14 Victoria Terrace, Abbey Village, Nr Chorley, Lancs. **Runners-up:** Samantha Hale (14), Ancaster House Cotts., Ermine Street, Ancaster, Nr Grantham, Lincs; Clair Louise Davis (13), Zostera, 15 Caudwell Close, Grove, Wantage, Oxon; Sonia Adams (14), 34 Spring Vale, Swanmore, Southampton, Hants; Cherri Dagger (15), 41 Oriel Grove, Southdown, Bath, Avon; Joanne Milne (13), The Croft, Canonbie, Dumfries and Galloway; Dianne Orban (15), Borreraig House, Morangie Road, Tain, Ross-shire, Scotland; Carol Huxley (14), Park Farm, Hawkesyard, Rugeley, Staffs; Jill Christine Evans (14), 429 London Road, Appleton, Warrington, Cheshire; Alison Berrieman (15), 40 St Peters Way, New Bradwell, Milton Keynes, Bucks; Clare Holstead (14), Maywood, 49 Bradbourne Road, Sevenoaks, Kent.

Juniors (aged 12 and under)

Winner: Leigh Harrison (12), 19 Lime Avenue, Luton, Beds. **Runners-up:** Carol Boress (12), 103 Bedford Road, Willington, Beds; Kirsty Sandbrook (8), 16 Barwell Grove, Emsworth, Hants; Jane Pears (12), Reedsford Farm, Mindrum, Northumberland; Clare Boxall (10), 32 Gypsy Lane, Gt Amwell, Ware, Herts; Anne-Marie Porteous (10), c/o 11 Park View Lane, Alston, Cumbria; Caroline Potts (8), Sisterpath Mill, Fogo, Duns, Berwickshire; Catherine Keeler (8), 3 Bridgefield Road, Tankerton, Whitstable, Kent; Nicola Jane Evans (11), 56 Long Barn Lane, Whitley, Reading, Berks; Emma Hopkins (9), Fairview, Defford, Worcester; Audrey Henderson (11), 33 Mayfield Road, Scone, Perth, Scotland.

The SATURDAY HIRELINGS

by Caroline Akrill
Illustrated by Elaine Roberts

"I suppose you think this is riding?" Charlotte said, half-turning in her saddle as she passed. "It isn't, of course."

"I can't think *what* you mean," Krisia replied in an irritated voice, hauling uselessly at the reins in a vain attempt to prevent her mount from resting its nose on the rump of Charlotte's elderly grey. "Of *course* this is riding. What else could it possibly be?"

"Well," Charlotte said, considering it, "you could call it nose-to-tailing, I suppose, or follow-my-leadering, but," she paused for a moment in order to apply her legs smartly to the grey mare without appreciable result, "it isn't *riding.* Not *proper* riding, it's just a substitute for the real thing; it's a charade, that's all."

"CHARLOTTE!" The instructor's voice shrilled indignantly from the centre of the manège. "You wouldn't actually be breaking one of our little rules, would you? You wouldn't actually be talking?"

"Of course I wouldn't," Charlotte agreed, adding for Krisia's benefit out of the corner of her mouth, "and I wouldn't actually be riding either."

"Krisia," her mother said. "Telephone."

"Well," Charlotte's firm voice announced. "I've done it. I've made the arrangements."

"What arrangements?" Krisia enquired, feeling apprehensive.

"Arrangements for some proper riding," Charlotte said. "Arrangements for The Real Thing. I've got two hirelings for the Saturday Meet. We're going hunting."

"But *Charles,*" Krisia said, appalled, "we've never hunted, and I can't possibly go. I'm anti-blood sports. I don't approve of hunting; I even signed a form!"

"Rubbish," Charlotte said dismissively. "In any case, who's to know that? Besides, they probably won't kill anything, I believe they hardly *ever* do."

"All the same," Krisia decided, "I'd rather not."

"Well, that's just *marvellous,* isn't it?" Charlotte declared in an exasperated voice. "You say you'd like to know what proper riding's like, you agree that we should experience The Real Thing for just once in our lives, you let me go ahead and make all the arrangements, and then you calmly turn round and say you'd rather not. Honestly, Krisia, that's really *great.*"

"Oh, Charles," Krisia said, repentant. "I'm sorry, truly I am."

There was a small tense silence, then Charlotte said in a stiff little voice, "Of course, if your principles mean more to you than our friendship . . ."

"They don't," Krisia said, but then, wanting to be truthful, she added, "at least, I don't think they do."

"And if you actually believe," Charlotte continued, "that in order to sit in judgement, you don't need to consider both points of view . . ."

"There is that way of looking at it, I suppose," Krisia admitted.

"Or to be able to speak from personal experience, not just hearsay . . ."

"You could be right," Krisia said with a sigh.

"I did find a very cheap yard," Charlotte pointed out. "I even managed to knock them down to fifteen pounds. They wanted twenty."

"Fifteen pounds doesn't sound all that expensive," Krisia said, although privately, even for a taste of The Real Thing, she thought it was a lot of money. She thought of her savings, totalling exactly that amount, painfully scraped together over the last six months towards a pair of ivory suede-seated breeches to go with her long rubber riding boots, and tucked securely into the pages of *Equitation for the Week-end Rider;* and so that Charlotte should realise the extent of her sacrifice, not only of principles but also of hard cash, in order to preserve the delicate balance of their friendship, she added, "Even so, seven pounds fifty is half of my savings."

"Not fifteen pounds for *two,* stupid," Charlotte said in disgust. "Fifteen pounds *each.*"

They stood at the appointed place in their thin, red-lined show jackets, hairnetted, rubber booted. It was exceedingly cold. Horseboxes, trailers and landrovers passed them by, each driver's throat stiffened by stock and pin.

"Charles," Krisia said, an edge of hope in her voice, "they will come?" She rather hoped they wouldn't.

"They said eleven," Charlotte said, looking

"Well, I've done it," Charlotte said in her firm voice. "I've got two hirelings for the Saturday Meet. We're going hunting."
"But *Charles,*" Krisia said, appalled. "We've never hunted, and I can't possibly go . . ."

at her watch, "it's only just gone that; and yes, they're sure to turn up – after all – thirty quid . . ."

A green cattle wagon, paint peeling, rattled along the lane and juddered to a halt in the lay-by opposite. A spotty youth with hair down to his shoulder blades jumped out of the cab, crashed down the ramp, yanked out sagging gates and vanished inside. When he reappeared he was dragging what appeared to be a moose. The moose was actually a faded bay horse with endless spindly legs, a sparse tail set upon hindquarters that dropped steeply away from a goose rump, a huge head with lop ears, a pronounced roman nose, and a hideously high wither set like a blade at the end of its short but ewe-shaped neck.

In spite of her nerves, and the cold, and the loss of the ivory suede-seated breeches, Krisia had to laugh. "Imagine, Charles," she said in a low voice, "having to appear out hunting on something like that!"

"Imagine hard," Charlotte said, taking her by the arm and propelling her towards the lay-by with a look of grievous discontent, "because I rather think that one's yours."

Krisia's boots squeaked a protest as her legs involuntarily stopped walking. "Oh, *Charles*," she said, aghast and rooted to the spot. "It can't be!"

The moose stepped down the ramp with elaborate care, pausing at the foot to survey its surroundings through slightly protuberant eyes. A vastly oversized noseband drooped over its whiskery nose, it wore a whitened browband, and its thin, bristly mane had been plaited in a

futile attempt at beautification. "Oh, Charles," Krisia moaned. "Why mine?"

There was now something of a to-do within the cattle wagon. Hooves, like gunfire, rattled against the sides. The spotty youth swore. The wagon rocked.

"Unless you prefer to take the other, of course," Charlotte offered with untypical generosity. "Although they did say," she added, as the youth was dragged down the ramp at breakneck speed by a wild-eyed, sweat-streaked chestnut, "that the bay horse with the white browband was the quietest."

"The Other" began to bounce up and down on the tarmac in a frenzy of anxiety with its head in the air and its tail held aloft like a banner. It wore a standing martingale with two knots in it and a long cheeked Pelham with a single rein attached to the bottom ring. Even Krisia, who knew nothing about bitting, thought this unpromising.

"Perhaps I'll stick with the bay," she said. "At least it looks dependable." This was true. The moose, its thyroid gaze fixed stolidly into the far distance, looked as if it might never move again.

The youth pulled a frayed halter off the chestnut's pitching head and held out his hand to Charlotte. "Money in advance," he said. They paid up in silence. The youth pocketed the money, handed them the horses, clambered back into the cab, turned the radio to full

volume, opened a can of beer and put his boots up on the windscreen, prepared to sit it out until their return.

They stood on the tarmac with the moose and the prancing chestnut. "Oh well," Charlotte said, shrugging her shoulders, "a cheap hireling is a cheap hireling, I suppose." She threw the reins over the chestnut's flickering ears and tightened its girth. The chestnut leapt in the air. Charlotte hung on to it, managing to pull on her gloves, adjust her hat and pull down her stirrup irons. She was not easily daunted.

Krisia regarded all this with wonder. "Do you suppose it ever stands still long enough to eat?" she enquired. "You can count every one of its ribs!"

"I should think it sweats everything off." Charlotte hopped across the lane after the chestnut, one foot firmly wedged in its stirrup. "If you ask me, it's hyper-active." She gained the saddle at last and the chestnut skittered back across the lane, showing the whites of its eyes. "Well, do come on," Charlotte said impatiently, "we don't want to be late."

Krisia turned back to the moose, half-envious of the chestnut, hyper-active or not. The moose was a fright. He was the ugliest horse she had ever seen in her life. She fumbled irritably with stiff girth straps, and pulled down stirrup irons whose treads had been worn smooth by years of use. "I should never have agreed to come," she thought. "I should never have been persuaded; I'm weak, that's my trouble." The moose stood like a stuffed exhibit as she heaved herself unwillingly into the saddle. The reins lay unattended on his gaunt neck as she tried to adjust the length of leathers whose holes didn't match. Charlotte shouted at her from away down the lane. The chestnut was proceeding sideways, like a crab, swishing its tail. "If this is The Real Thing," Krisia thought savagely, "I'll make do with the substitute. The charade will suit me just fine."

Bitterly resenting the loss of the ivory suede-seated breeches, lost in unworthy exchange for a day which could only go from bad to worse, Krisia picked up the reins and kicked the moose in the ribs. The moose immediately lifted his head and sprang into an unrecognisable gait, neither walk nor trot, yet surprisingly comfortable to sit to. "Charles!" Krisia shouted. "You might at least *wait!*"

A gaggle of Pony Club members passed by, tweed-coated, their ponies trace-clipped, cantering purposefully along the grass verge. The chestnut jumped in the air at their approach and made after them in a series of kangaroo hops. Charlotte held on grimly. She looked rather hot. The moose rocked on regardless, his lop ears held at right-angles. Krisia leaned forward hesitantly, and patted his faded neck.

Round a bend they came suddenly upon the Meet, a milling throng of horses, hounds and people, shot with scarlet. Charlotte hauled the chestnut to a halt with its head in the air and its

back legs sliding apart, not at all the kind of thing one could get away with at the manège. "We'll stand here," she panted. "I don't want to get mixed up with that lot." No sooner had she uttered the words than the entire Meet gathered itself together and swept past them as they stood. The chestnut flew backwards and dropped its hind legs into a ditch. Charlotte fell soundly upon its neck and banged her nose. The horse scrambled out of the ditch with a large trailing bramble attached to its tail. It whipped round, unable to endure it.

Meanwhile, the moose looked on in mild interest as hounds flooded the lane with lemon and white, and the hunt servants clattered past with the smartest subscribers mounted on expensive thoroughbred horses hard on their heels. Charlotte flung herself out of the saddle and grabbed at the trailing bramble, her nose already swollen, her eyes watering and her face scarlet with embarrassment.

"Well," Krisia enquired, as they fell in behind the Pony Club members at a rib-rattling trot, the chestnut leaping and barging, the moose settling into a long, effortless lope, "are you enjoying your taste of The Real Thing?"

"Of course I'm enjoying it," Charlotte snapped. "What an idiotic question to ask."

The first draw was a wind-swept thicket on the side of a hill. The sky was leaden. The wind cut like a knife. The chestnut fidgeted about across the ride, white socks dancing, upslung head straining the knotted martingale to its limits, eyes fixed on the hound-filled thicket, ears pointing forward like a terrier. One of a group of well-heeled followers was heard to make a caustic remark about people who used single rein Pelhams.

"What would he like me to do, I wonder," Charlotte said angrily, "put the rein on the top ring and break my neck?"

"I've really no idea," Krisia said innocently. The moose had backed firmly into the best shelter the thicket afforded and was holding fast.

The Gone Away, when it happened, seemed to take everyone unawares. Where there had previously been silence, there was now the sound of horn and hounds, and galloping hooves and snorting breath; and where there had previously been almost no movement at all, there were suddenly flying hounds and galloping horses everywhere. Charlotte was carried away in the first flight, helpless as a leaf in the wind.

A ditch loomed, deep and bramble-filled. The chestnut flew up to it, stopped, and teetered on the edge in a torment of indecision. Charlotte, not knowing which might be worse, to stop or to go on, applied her stick. Overcome

with astonishment, the chestnut jumped high into the air and plummeted into the brambly depths. The horse leaped and hopped through it somehow, carrying Charlotte, yelling, scratched, agonised, her jodhpurs a mass of pulled threads, and hurled itself at the opposite bank, gaining the brink and dashing on without a pause, whilst Charlotte fought to stay in the saddle, grabbing at reins soaked and slimy with sweat. "Oh, you *beast*," she cried. "You absolute BEAST!"

Not far behind, the moose gathered its loose limbs together and sailed over the ditch, settling himself into a steady, undemanding, yet relentless gallop, gaining upon other horses better looking, better bred and probably, Krisia thought, feeling a surge of affection for the faded old bay horse, younger and better fed then he.

Some way ahead, she could see that the chestnut's headlong flight had been arrested by a low, thick, cut-and-laid hedge. Charlotte set the plunging horse at it again and again, only to have it swerve out into the path of oncoming riders.

"*Charles!*" Krisia shouted urgently. "Follow me! The moose jumps like a *stag!*"

The moose thudded steadily towards the hedge, launched himself into the air and landed without even breaking his stride. "Oh!" Krisia cried joyfully, leaning forward in order to throw her arms around his threadbare neck. "You *are* a clever old thing!" She turned in her saddle in time to see the chestnut land with a mighty grunt, bringing a good deal of blackthorn to ground with its back legs.

Soon she and Charlotte were galloping abreast, the wind tugging at their cheeks, the thunder of hooves in their ears. Little knots of riders hurtled along to their left and to their right. Hounds and their attendant scarlet coats were clearly to be seen two fields ahead.

Krisia, her principles and her ivory suede-seated breeches well and truly forgotten, was suddenly overcome by the sheer splendour of it. "Oh, Charles!" she said with a whoop. "Isn't proper riding *wonderful!*"

Charlotte, still intent on regaining her stirrups after the cut-and-laid, shot her a vengeful look, seemed about to make an angry retort, and then suddenly, unexpectedly, she began to laugh.

They galloped, on their Saturday hirelings, stirrup by stirrup, and as the chestnut's stride steadied at last to match the rhythmic, loping, stride of the moose, they looked at each other, and they laughed and laughed and laughed.

"Oh, *Charles*," Krisia gasped helplessly, as the wind dried the tears to salt upon her cheeks, "I'm *so* glad we came!"

STARS OF THE FUTURE

MATTHEW LANNI   by Lesley Eccles

A sense of humour and the ability to keep your cool are useful qualities for any young show jumper and they are certainly possessed by Matthew Lanni.

Success has been following Matthew around the show circuit but, chatting to him, it is obvious that all this has not gone to his head.

Although it is the rider who gets all the glory, this lively young man is quick to point out that his family's support is an essential ingredient for success.

Everyone pitches in, but Matthew's respect for his father booms out. "I'm lucky with my Dad – he decides everything and he knows which horses are going to be good for me."

When he is on the road touring the shows, both Mum and Dad help out and his sister, Sarah, takes charge of the horses and ponies. Since the mid '70s Matthew has been competing seriously.

He started affiliated classes at the tender age of nine, jumping with just one pony at first. Then he started to build up a string and by 1979 he had a JA and a JC pony. He soon upgraded the second string to his bow and there were other JC ponies to follow on.

Ponies came into his father's yard, some of them to be sold on, so Matthew had about five ponies on which he competed seriously.

Holmsley Lady is the one mount that does not belong to the family and the pony had won nothing until Matthew took her on four years ago. Now she is a JA pony.

Ponies have been part of Matthew's life right from the beginning, and he cannot remember the first time he clambered into the saddle!

His Pony Club days were with the Badsworth branch and close links still exist because the Pony Club uses the facilities at the Lannis' home.

Matthew is grateful for the opportunities he has had – good facilities and plenty of ponies with his father as his guide – but he still has a level-headed, commonsense outlook.

Recognising that getting to the top in show jumping is a tough, uphill climb he has stayed on at school to take Advanced levels. Then, with a good education to fall back on if necessary, "I am going to see if I can really be good enough to succeed in show jumping."

Life is very hectic but Matthew has a diversity of interests and crams football into an already full schedule. A local club and his school team call on his services regularly.

Apart from that there is not much time for other hobbies and, as his father says, if you're going to do something well you have to really apply yourself to the job. So that's just what Matthew does – successfully, too.

He was a member of the victorious British team in the 1982 European Pony Championships in Copenhagen, and he looks upon this gold medal as one of his two major achievements. His career has also taken him to Germany with the pony show jumping team.

The other milestone in his life was an individual victory – winning the Whitbread Young Riders Championship in the same year at the Horse of the Year Show. Matthew is among the few young riders to have qualified both a pony and a horse for Wembley.

In the Young Riders Championship it was his 16.2 h.h. chestnut mare, Penny Farthing, who brought him the honours.

This is where keeping cool really came into play because he was last to go and there had been no clear rounds. A wise, steady, faultless round in excellent style gave him the title.

Matthew is a modest, amenable teenager and I am sure that whatever success comes his way, he will still be the same as he is now.

MICHELLE AND ANNETTE LEWIS

by Linda Burgess

When the Lewis sisters take to the show jumping circuit each season, fellow competitors have to look to their laurels. For Michelle and Annette have only one aim in mind – to reach the top of the show jumping tree and stay there.

Horses have always been a part of the Lewis family life. The two girls never compete at a show without the support of their parents, Shirley and Alan, brother Anthony and, when her own family commitments allow, elder sister Jacqueline.

Success for the sisters came early. Both carried off prizes as members of the Essex Hunt South Pony Club, and Annette, or Nettie as the family call her, was picking up the rosettes in lead-rein classes on a super Prince Philip Cup Games pony called Cherie. By all accounts, Cherie, at 35 years of age, is quite a character. The only way the girls can catch her is to tempt her with a pint of milk in a bucket!

By the time she was four years old, Nettie had made the headlines in her local paper – for competing at shows on Jackie's horse, a 16.2 h.h. piebald named Apache.

Adagio, a 13.2 h.h. strawberry roan, gave Michelle her first sweet taste of success. It was on this pony that Michelle gained a third placing in a 13.2 h.h. championship class at Hickstead. Adagio eventually became one of the country's top 13.2 h.h. ponies.

Other ponies came and went, each adding a few more mementoes to the sisters' ever-increasing trophy case.

But life hasn't always been an easy path for the Lewises who have had more than their fair share of tragedies.

The first cruel blow struck when Crown Court, one of two super ponies the family has fond memories of, died from a twisted gut. This pony won numerous county championships and a junior class at the Royal International Show. A few days after winning this class, Crown Court was to have competed at Bicton – sadly, he never did.

Three years ago, Michelle badly damaged her back following an accident with a horse named Ironside. The family thought she would never walk again, let alone ride and compete at international level.

On the day that Michelle was undergoing an operation to her back, fate struck another blow. A promising young showjumper named Khan was being exercised when he was involved in a collision with a lorry and had to be destroyed.

pictures courtesy of Horse & Pony Magazine

From then on things just had to get better. And they did.

Both sisters have competed at international level and have represented their country. Michelle has carried the flag three times as a member of the British Team in Junior European competitions. In 1981, together with Zoe Bates, Mark Heffer, Lesley McNaught and Maria Green, she took part in the Junior European Championships at Aarau in Switzerland. The young riders came home with the individual and team golds, and won the European Pony Championships.

Michelle has also laid claim to the National Young Rider of 1981 title with her top horse, Pascal.

For many, success goes to their heads. Not so with Michelle and Annette, who are down-to-earth, lively girls with tremendous enthusiasm and a sense of commitment to their 'job'.

"Our only ambition is to be the top riders in the show jumping world – and we will," said the sisters confidently.

MY VERY OWN PONY

Can I afford it?

Well, can you? We take a look at the costs of keeping a pony in an effort to find the answer.

Of course you want a pony. Who doesn't? A pony of your own is more than a mere possession. He is the passport to a new, exciting and wonderful world, the means of making friends, a constant source of joy – and, regrettably, expense.

It is far better both for you and the pony to have some ideas of the costs involved in maintaining a pony before you embark on the great adventure of buying one to keep. It will save a lot of heartbreak in the long run.

The first thing to face up to is that a pony's needs will far outstrip your weekly pocket money, unless you have madly extravagant and indulgent parents, in which case financial considerations are the least of your worries.

But few of us are in that happy position. Most of us have to take the pleasure of owning a pony very seriously indeed. However, the fact that there are around 50,000 members of the Pony Club, of whom the great majority do own their own ponies, does suggest that the problems are not insuperable.

When discussing with your family the possibility of getting a pony, it helps to do your homework properly. Your parents – who may well have to make some sacrifices themselves in order to give you your heart's desire – will be both impressed and reassured if you can show them how sensibly you have approached the whole subject.

So here, to help you, is some idea of what it costs to have a pony of your own.

The money paid out on a pony can be divided into capital outlay and running costs. The first, of course, is a one-off item and should not have to be repeated until you progress to a second pony. Even then, most of it will come back to you when you sell the first pony, and you might even make a profit if you are a good, competitive rider and have made the pony more valuable than when you first acquired it.

Capital outlay covers such items as the pony itself, saddlery and clothing, grooming equipment, feed storage bins and buckets, and possibly a loose box or field shelter.

Running costs are: rent of field or stable, food, shoeing, veterinary bills, insurance, show entries and transport to and from shows, riding instruction and, of course, your Pony Club subscription. Let us take each item of running costs in turn.

Rent of field or stable Unless your family owns a field and/or stable, you will have to rent one. You will need a minimum of 1½–2 acres on which to keep a pony permanently, but remember that the smaller the pasture the less productive it will be, getting poached and muddy in winter and dry and grassless in summer. If you are able to rent more than one field, you will be able to use them in turn.

Ponies are selective and wasteful grazers, taking more out of a field than they put into it, so it is important to preserve your pasture as much as you can. An overgrazed field can become horse-sick, riddled with worms and full of the coarse, rank grasses which horses will not eat. Regular removal of droppings or putting sheep or cattle on to the pasture will deal with the first problem, rest and a mid-summer cut will help with the second.

Most people try to share a field with other horse owners. This way, your pony will have company – vitally important to the happiness of horses – and you may find that it cuts the costs as well.

Field rents vary enormously, even within the same locality, although much depends on supply and demand. If you are lucky and can find a farmer who likes horses or a landowner who gets pleasure from seeing a pony in his paddock, you could pay as little as 50p or £1 a week. But £3 is more usual and £5 or more is not unknown. Expect to double the amount if you hire a stable as well. If the rent is low, however, you will probably be expected to maintain the gate and fencing and, depending on their condition to start with, this could mean some capital expenditure later on.

Food for the pony In summer, when the grass is nutritious and growing well, a field-kept pony will be able to do light work on a diet of grass alone. In winter, however, even if he is only being hacked gently at weekends, he must be given hay. Not just a handful or two when you think about it, but a daily ration of between 10 and 12 lb, according to his size, more when the weather is very severe.

The cheapest way of buying hay is direct from the farmer 'off the field' – that is, purchasing it as soon as haymaking is finished and it is baled ready for storage. New hay like this is sold by the ton and costs about £40. Each ton contains some 40 bales and each bale weighs about 56 lb. A 12 to 12 h.h. pony will need roughly a ton of hay to see him through the winter from November to April.

But the bulk buying of hay does need adequate storage. If hay is stored outside, even on a platform and protected by a tarpaulin, some of the hay will not be fit to eat before the winter comes to an end.

If you only have storage room for, say, six bales, you will have to buy it at regular intervals, either privately or from a corn merchants. The price will depend on how much hay is available but will not be less than £1.50 a bale.

Then there are the hard feeds which keep a pony fit, give him energy and make him capable of doing the work you expect from him. In winter, good supplementary feeds are sugar beet pulp, which must be soaked in water for 24 hours before it is fed, and barley, either crushed or boiled. Both these help to keep flesh on a pony that is wintering out and give him internal protection in cold and wet weather. Both should be mixed with broad bran before feeding.

Pony nuts, oats and any of the proprietary brands of special mixtures available at feed merchants may be offered to the pony in work, to give him energy.

All these feeds cost around £4 per 25-kilogram bag, and a daily ration of soaked sugar beet, bran and nuts, weighing 3 to 4lb, will produce a feed bill, not counting hay, of about £15 every four weeks.

Take expert advice on quantities, as hard foods can make ponies excitable.

Bedding Stable-kept ponies need some form of bedding, which can be composed of straw (wheat straw is best), woodshavings, peat or paper. These are sold in bale form and it pays to shop around and to buy in bulk, if you can. A sum of about £15 should cover your monthly needs.

TABLE OF ANNUAL RUNNING COSTS

Pony	12.2 h.h. living out all the year round	13.2 h.h. at d-i-y livery for £10 a week	14.2 h.h. out in the day, stabled at night
	£	£	£
Field rent	150		150
Stable rent	—		150
Bedding	—	520	120
Hay	50		100
Short feeds	90	120	180
Shoeing	80	100	120
Vet's bills	30	30	30
Insurance	25	35	45
Show entries	30	40	50
Transport	30	50	50
Hunting	10	20	50
Instruction	75	100	100
PC membership	7	7	7
PC camp	50	50	50
TOTAL	**£627**	**£1072**	**£1202**

A pony wintering out may need a New Zealand rug, especially if it is partially clipped.

Livery If it is impossible for you to look after your pony entirely on your own, you could keep him at a livery stables. Charges range from do-it-yourself at around £7 a week to £20 or more. In the first case, you will probably have to provide the food yourself; in the latter, the stables are likely to include the cost of food and bedding in the overall price.

Shoeing Even if your pony has good, hard feet and your riding is almost exclusively on soft ground, so that you can safely leave your pony without shoes, you will still need a visit from the blacksmith every four to six weeks so that the hooves can be trimmed and kept in shape. Most Pony Club ponies, however, will need shoes and they have to be renewed regularly. A farrier charges from £10 to £20 a set of shoes. If he is VAT registered, there will be an extra 15 per cent on top of that. Your annual shoeing bill, therefore, will be around £80–100.

Veterinary bills Just because your pony is *never* ill, don't imagine that there will be no veterinary expenses. Regular worming is a must and should be carried out at the intervals recommended by the makers of the product you use, if you want to keep your healthy pony fit and alert. There are various worming products on the market, which are administered in powder or paste form.

Vaccination against tetanus is another must. Tetanus germs live in the soil and can enter the pony's body through a cut, especially puncture wounds. The cut may be so small that you have not even noticed it, but a pony with lockjaw has only a 50 per cent chance of recovery. Fortunately, vaccination gives lifelong immunity provided that booster injections are administered annually. The cost of a vet's visit seems a small price to pay for so great a protection.

Close contact between a stabled pony and its young owner builds up a lasting friendship.

Vaccination against equine influenza is also important, and may be essential if your Pony Club branch holds functions at local racecourses or equitation centres. Racecourses in particular will not allow any horse or pony on their premises without a current 'flu vaccination certificate.

The 'flu and anti-tetanus injections may be combined in one dose.

Insurance You can insure your pony against loss through theft, death or permanent injury. You can insure against heavy vet's bills (usually excluding the first £25) and against your tack being stolen. Most policies include personal liability cover in case your pony injures someone and you find yourself being sued for damages. Premiums cost from £20 to £50 a year, depending on the value of the pony and the amount of cover you require. It is worth remembering, however, that membership of the Pony Club automatically insures you against third party risks.

Show entries and transport Even if you only go to shows which are near enough to hack to, the cost of entry fees soon mounts up. Gymkhana events cost about 40–50p each to enter, unaffiliated jumping and showing classes £1.25 to £3. Most people compete for the fun of entering and the chance to win a rosette, although some shows give money prizes. In an average season, you will probably want to go to about ten shows, hunter trials and one-day events, at a cost of about £30 in entry fees. A day's hunting would set you back between £5 and £10.

Success in your local shows will almost certainly encourage you to enter ones further from home. If you can share transport with other entrants, the hire of a box and driver would amount to about £10. Your parents, however, may decide to buy a trailer (capital expenditure around £700) but a car drawing a trailer uses more petrol than it normally does and this contributes to the running costs of keeping a pony.

Riding instruction Membership of the Pony Club entitles you to attend working rallies where expert instruction is given free of charge. Many children, however, like to continue with regular riding lessons after they have acquired a pony. A fortnightly lesson on your own pony, perhaps in company with one or two others, costs from £3 to £5 an hour.

Membership of the Pony Club The £7 annual subscription represents remarkable value. Due in October each year, it provides you with free access to a wide variety of activities and unlimited advice on the care of your pony. Pony Club camp, always popular with PC members, may cost up to £50, but in many branches is considerably less.

Depressed? There is no real need to be. Any hobby costs money and few interests are as absorbing and enjoyable as caring for a pony. The secret is to know beforehand how much your family can afford and to choose the pony best suited to your financial position. After that, the amount you spend is up to you.

A field shelter is a good place in which to hang a haynet. You will find that a pony uses the shelter more often in summer than in winter.

GALLOP INTO BREAKFAST

Surprisingly, there are times when you and your pony are apart. Maybe your pony is resting or perhaps it is a wet afternoon and you have finished cleaning your tack. To fill in those spare moments, here are some ideas for presents for your friends – or for yourself, designed by Geoffrey Hemming.

If you think boiled-eggs on the breakfast table look boring here's a simple idea to brighten them up – cover them with a pony egg cosy.

To make the cosy, just collect:

Cardboard egg carton cup
White cardboard
Paints
Glue

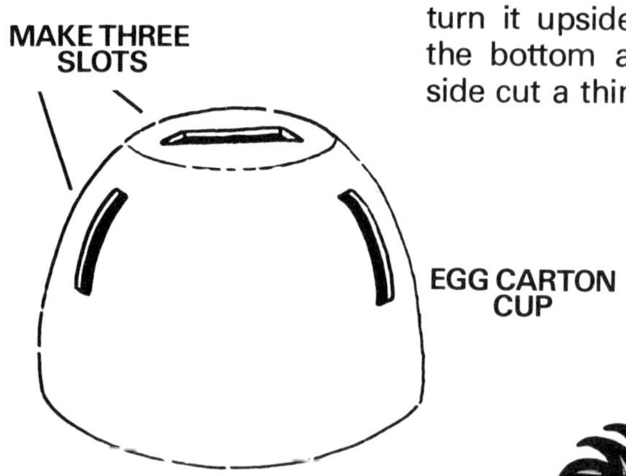

MAKE THREE SLOTS

Remove one cup from a cardboard egg carton and turn it upside down. Across the bottom and down each side cut a thin slot.

EGG CARTON CUP

On white cardboard draw the pony's head and front legs and cut out.

BEND

WHITE CARDBOARD

Glue the end of the pony's neck into the slot in the base of the cup and the two legs into the side slots. Now paint the pony egg cosy in bright colours and leave to dry. When dry enough to touch, bend both legs so that they fold down in front of the body.

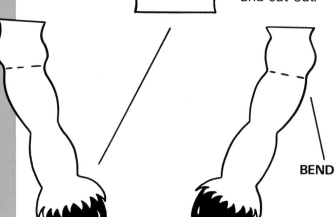

Your pony egg cover is now complete. Use it next time you have boiled eggs for breakfast and you'll really start the day with a gallop!

MAKE A PONY PIN DRAWER

Do you have to hunt high and low every time you need a safety-pin? The problem can easily be solved by making yourself a pony pin drawer. You'll know exactly where the pins are then and you won't waste time looking for them!

To make the drawer, collect:

Two match-boxes
Sheet of white cardboard
Crayons or paints
Two paper pins
Glue
Wool

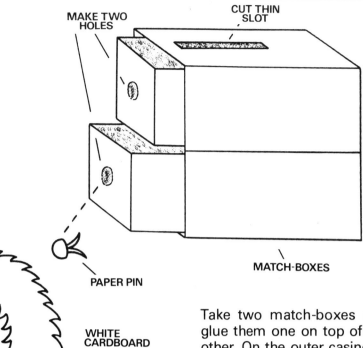

MAKE TWO HOLES

CUT THIN SLOT

PAPER PIN

MATCH-BOXES

WHITE CARDBOARD

Take two match-boxes and glue them one on top of the other. On the outer casing of the top match-box cut a thin slot. Make a small hole in each of the drawers and insert a paper pin. Open out the prongs on the inside. The paper pins serve as handles.

Cover the match-boxes on all sides, except where the drawers open out, with white cardboard and colour with paints or crayons. Draw the pony's head and cut out. Fold a piece of cardboard in half and on one side draw the front and back legs. Cut out through the folded card and you'll have a pair of both legs. Colour all parts with paints or crayons. Glue the base of the neck into the slot and the legs on to the sides of the drawer.

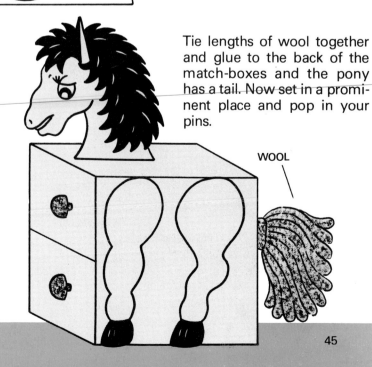

WOOL

Tie lengths of wool together and glue to the back of the match-boxes and the pony has a tail. Now set in a prominent place and pop in your pins.

PONIES AT RISK

Most of what your pony eats does him good. But there are some plants which could poison him. It is important to learn to recognise them and make sure your pony is safe.

Ponies graze on a wide variety of grasses and plants. Some are more nutritious than others, and some, like the flowers of thistles, are clearly regarded by ponies as a treat. A few plants, however, are poisonous.

Cases of ponies being fatally poisoned are fortunately rare. This is because the sensible and conscientious owner makes certain that a pony cannot get at dangerous plants, either by fencing them off or by removing them from the field and burning them.

Make sure your pony is safe by learning to identify the plants which could do him harm, and inspect your pony's field regularly to see that no toxic plant is growing within his reach.

The most dangerous plant of all is YEW. All parts of this common tree are poisonous — leaves, fruit and bark. If a yew tree is growing near the field, it must be securely and *widely* fenced off, widely enough not merely to prevent the pony from reaching over and nibbling it but to ensure that twigs and branches cannot be blown into the field during a gale. Yew contains a poison which causes heart failure and it acts too quickly for treatment to be given.

A common plant, often found on poor pasture, is RAGWORT. Luckily, this tall-growing weed with its bright yellow flowers is easy to spot and easy to remove. You will see it growing in clumps in mid-summer and that is the time to tackle it, before it has time to seed, by pulling it up by the roots, taking it out of the field and burning it.

Never leave dead ragwort lying around in the field as it is more dangerous dead than alive. Ponies usually ignore it when it is green and growing. The poison of ragwort is slow-acting with a cumulative effect, eventually destroying the liver.

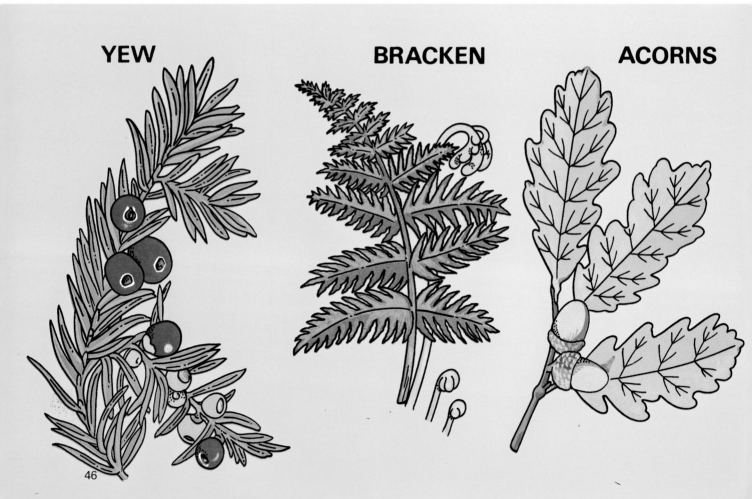

YEW　　　BRACKEN　　　ACORNS

Members of the henbane family – DEADLY NIGHT-SHADE, THORNAPPLE, WOODY NIGHTSHADE, GARDEN NIGHTSHADE and WILD TOBACCO – contain poisons which act on the nervous system. They are, however, less risky than other poisonous plants because they taste bitter and a pony would have to be very hungry before he ate them.

BRACKEN can be poisonous if ponies graze for long periods on the young shoots. It has a cumulative effect but this disappears if the pony is taken off pasture where bracken is growing. It is a common plant on hill pastures. There is no need to worry, however, if your pony snatches a quick bite of bracken while you are out riding.

ACORNS have to be eaten in large quantities before their toxic effect is noticed (the pony loses his appetite, becomes dull and listless, suffers from constipation, followed by diarrhoea). If your pony's field contains a number of oak trees, it is worth checking the ground beneath them after a gale and raking up the acorns. New Forest ponies, however, especially if they are Forest-bred, appear to have an immunity to acorn-poisoning.

Where your field is bordered by the gardens of houses, check to see that there are no ornamental shrubs within reach of the fence. If necessary, build an inner fence to keep the pony safe. Common shrubs, like BOX, PRIVET and LAUREL, can be poisonous, especially if clippings have been allowed to fall into the field.

One problem that many pony-owners have to face in this connection is to prevent well-meaning neighbours from tipping their lawn mowings into the pony's field. Newly cut grass smells so delicious that non-horsey people are convinced that they are giving the pony a treat. The pony regards it as a treat, too, and will guzzle away at grass-cuttings with gusto. Unfortunately, the mowings heat up and start decomposing very quickly, giving the pony indigestion and colic. Best to suggest tactfully to your neighbour that a few carrots, sliced into finger-shaped pieces so that they cannot cause choking, would do your pony far more good.

Other hazards which your pony may have to face, especially if a public footpath runs near his field, are plastic bags, broken bottles and tin cans. He could cut himself on broken glass and the jagged edges of cans or eat a plastic bag. Always keep a sharp look-out for litter and make a regular tour of the field. The time spent is well worth while.

And remember that it is the hungry pony who is most at risk. The best safeguard against accidental poisoning is to make certain that your pony has enough good grass or hay to eat at all times.

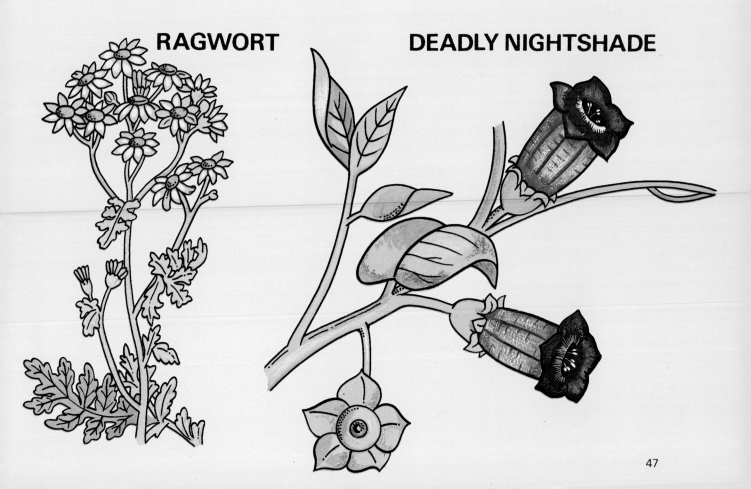

RAGWORT   **DEADLY NIGHTSHADE**

BUILDING YOUR OWN JUMPS

A course of jumps for you to practise over at home could make all the difference to you and your pony. George Mason, a Pony Club parent, describes how he set about building some fences for his daughter and her friends.

A full set of show jumps is expensive to buy and few of you have parents rich enough to equip you with all the jumps you would no doubt like to have. My own daughter was in just that situation so I decided to see how many jumps I could make at home. Of course, it helps to have a grown-up around who is handy with a hammer and saw.

One way of cutting the costs is to get an illustrated catalogue of show jumps and to copy the supports and wing stands as best you can. But this can still work out expensive if the wood has to be bought at a timber yard.

Before putting your hand into your pocket, see how much jump material you are able to collect. Many industrial sites and factories have old pallets lying around. Every so often, they collect up the discarded pallets and burn them. A polite word with the foreman will usually persuade him to put aside two or three pallets which are not too badly damaged. As long as you take them away, he will probably be quite happy to let you have them for nothing.

Demolition sites are another source of discarded timber. Again it is a matter of contacting the foreman, using all your charm, and you will no doubt be allowed to pick through the wood earmarked for a bonfire.

Old oil drums can be used to make jump stands or as jumps and fillers themselves. Once they have finished with the contents, factories often have no further need for the containers and are willing to give them away or to sell them for a few pence. Paint them bright colours and you are well on your way to building up an interesting jumping course.

Ask a neighbouring farmer if he has any liquid fertiliser or chemical containers to spare. These are made of plastic or metal and make useful holders for a series of jumping poles. You can vary the height by placing them on their sides or standing them upright. Remember to rinse them out thoroughly first, however, and give them stability by half-filling them with water.

I started off with a number of show jumps of the knock-down variety and the first drawings show how I used the types of materials I have mentioned.

Last summer, however, I was asked to help build a novice cross-country course for our Pony Club branch. It was designed to encourage the younger members with small ponies, and none of the jumps was too difficult or too frightening for them to tackle. We had a large number of larch poles at our disposal, a couple of telegraph poles and several straw bales.

We were able to leave some of the fences as permanent fixtures, but most of the jumps had to be removed at the end of the day.

The rest of the drawings show some of the different jumps we were able to make. Most of them could easily be adapted to give you some practice cross-country fences in your own paddock.

1a. Plastic containers come in various sizes. Rinse them well before half-filling them with water to give them stability.

1b. Use the containers, either upright or on their sides, to make a jumping grid – useful for schooling.

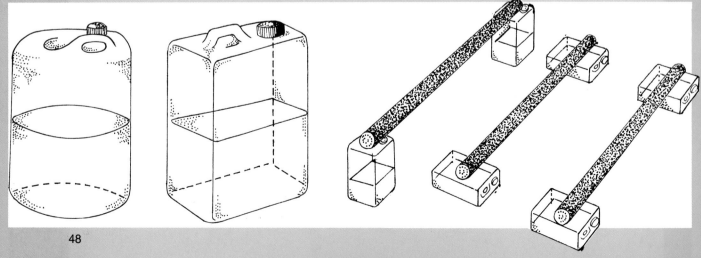

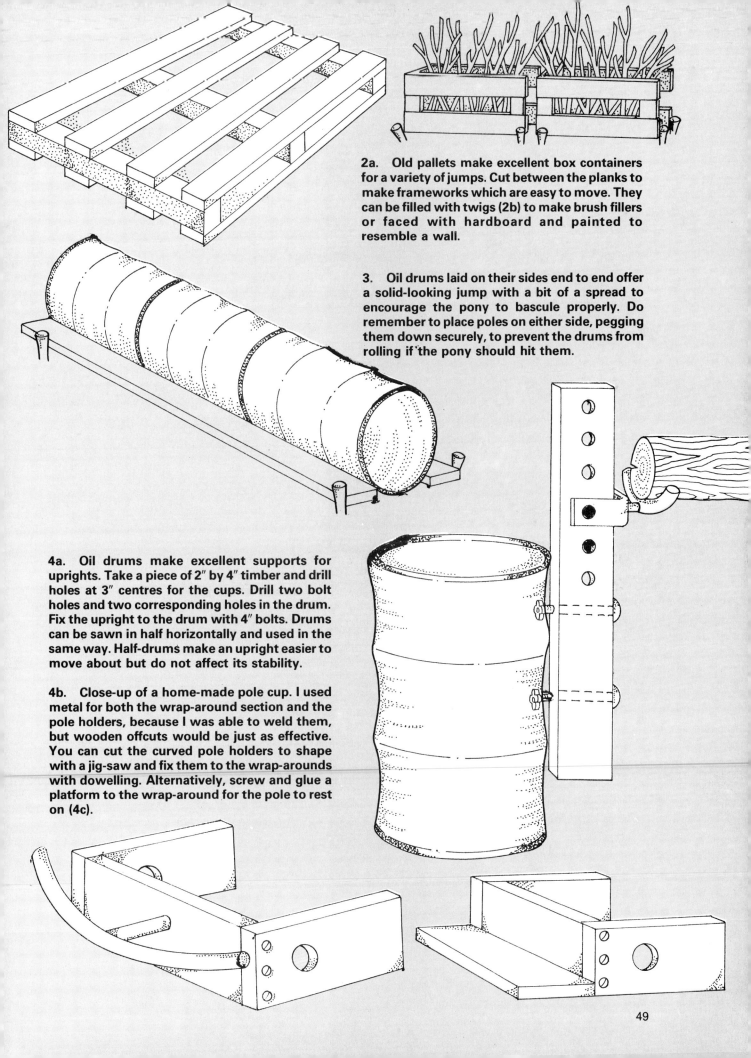

2a. Old pallets make excellent box containers for a variety of jumps. Cut between the planks to make frameworks which are easy to move. They can be filled with twigs (2b) to make brush fillers or faced with hardboard and painted to resemble a wall.

3. Oil drums laid on their sides end to end offer a solid-looking jump with a bit of a spread to encourage the pony to bascule properly. Do remember to place poles on either side, pegging them down securely, to prevent the drums from rolling if the pony should hit them.

4a. Oil drums make excellent supports for uprights. Take a piece of 2" by 4" timber and drill holes at 3" centres for the cups. Drill two bolt holes and two corresponding holes in the drum. Fix the upright to the drum with 4" bolts. Drums can be sawn in half horizontally and used in the same way. Half-drums make an upright easier to move about but do not affect its stability.

4b. Close-up of a home-made pole cup. I used metal for both the wrap-around section and the pole holders, because I was able to weld them, but wooden offcuts would be just as effective. You can cut the curved pole holders to shape with a jig-saw and fix them to the wrap-arounds with dowelling. Alternatively, screw and glue a platform to the wrap-around for the pole to rest on (4c).

49

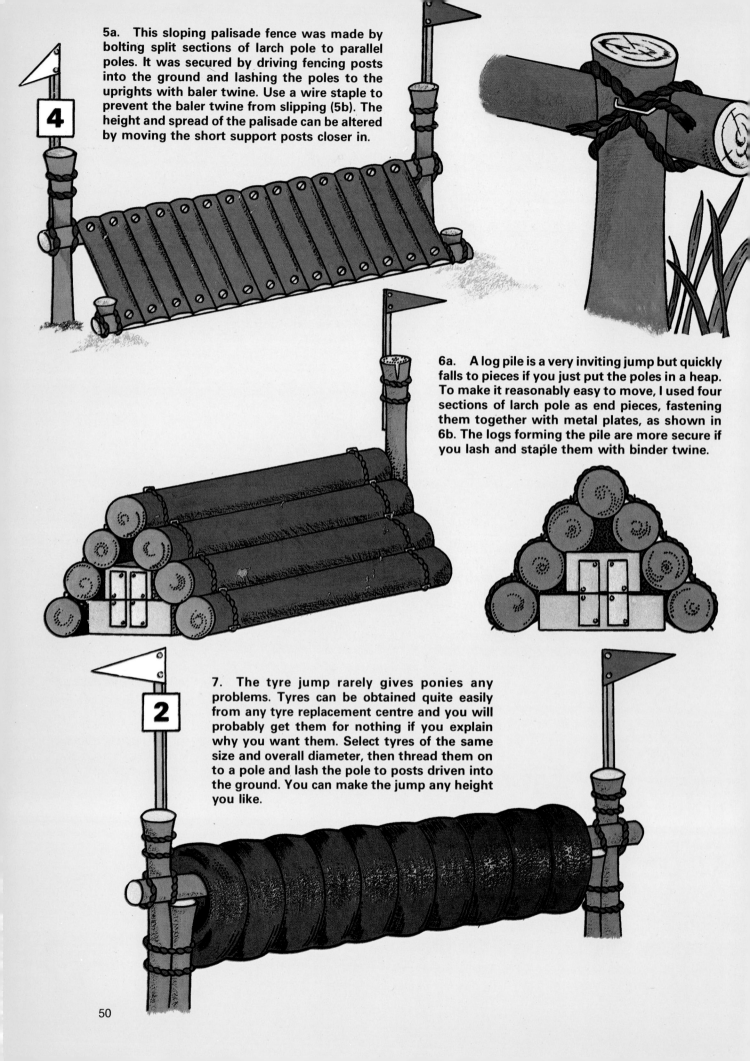

5a. This sloping palisade fence was made by bolting split sections of larch pole to parallel poles. It was secured by driving fencing posts into the ground and lashing the poles to the uprights with baler twine. Use a wire staple to prevent the baler twine from slipping (5b). The height and spread of the palisade can be altered by moving the short support posts closer in.

6a. A log pile is a very inviting jump but quickly falls to pieces if you just put the poles in a heap. To make it reasonably easy to move, I used four sections of larch pole as end pieces, fastening them together with metal plates, as shown in 6b. The logs forming the pile are more secure if you lash and staple them with binder twine.

7. The tyre jump rarely gives ponies any problems. Tyres can be obtained quite easily from any tyre replacement centre and you will probably get them for nothing if you explain why you want them. Select tyres of the same size and overall diameter, then thread them on to a pole and lash the pole to posts driven into the ground. You can make the jump any height you like.

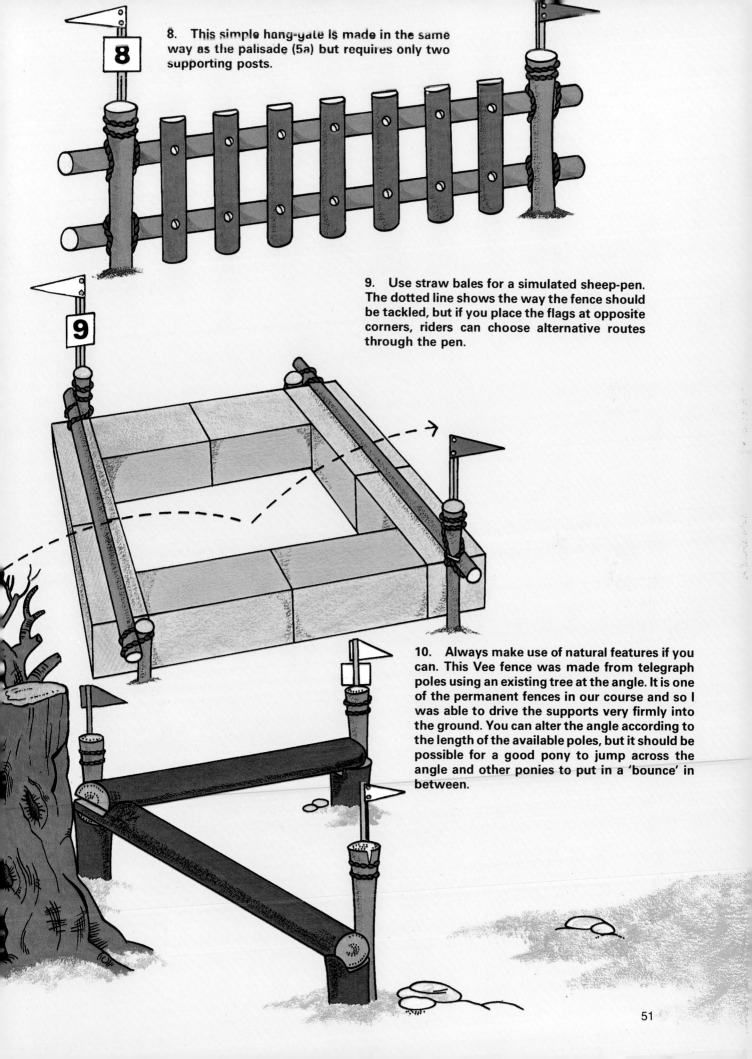

8. This simple hang-gate is made in the same way as the palisade (5a) but requires only two supporting posts.

9. Use straw bales for a simulated sheep-pen. The dotted line shows the way the fence should be tackled, but if you place the flags at opposite corners, riders can choose alternative routes through the pen.

10. Always make use of natural features if you can. This Vee fence was made from telegraph poles using an existing tree at the angle. It is one of the permanent fences in our course and so I was able to drive the supports very firmly into the ground. You can alter the angle according to the length of the available poles, but it should be possible for a good pony to jump across the angle and other ponies to put in a 'bounce' in between.

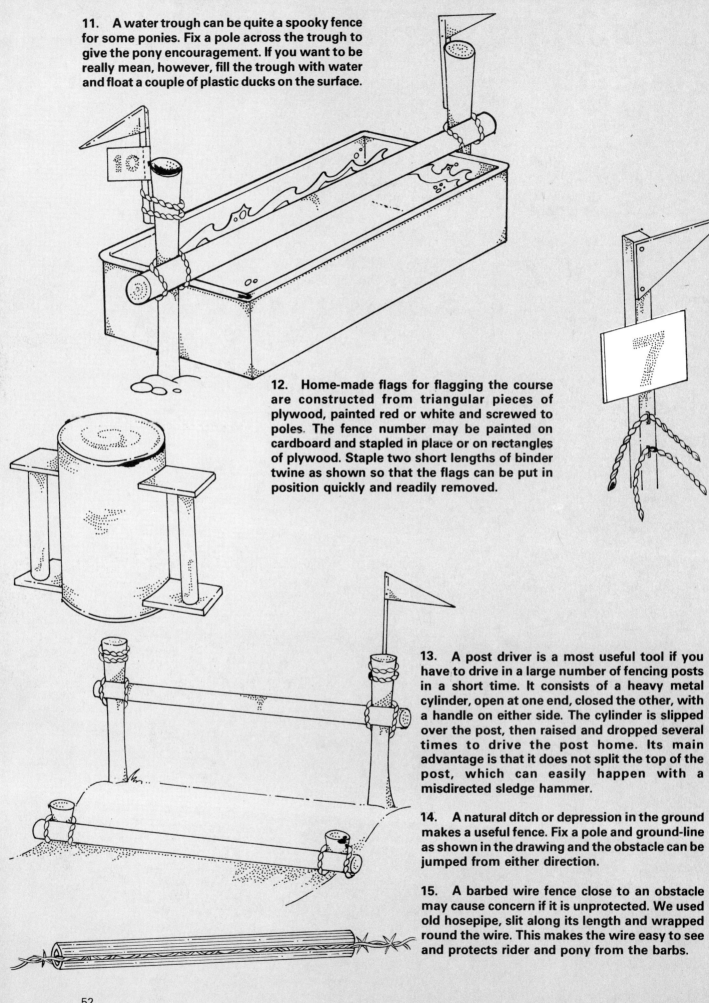

11. A water trough can be quite a spooky fence for some ponies. Fix a pole across the trough to give the pony encouragement. If you want to be really mean, however, fill the trough with water and float a couple of plastic ducks on the surface.

12. Home-made flags for flagging the course are constructed from triangular pieces of plywood, painted red or white and screwed to poles. The fence number may be painted on cardboard and stapled in place or on rectangles of plywood. Staple two short lengths of binder twine as shown so that the flags can be put in position quickly and readily removed.

13. A post driver is a most useful tool if you have to drive in a large number of fencing posts in a short time. It consists of a heavy metal cylinder, open at one end, closed the other, with a handle on either side. The cylinder is slipped over the post, then raised and dropped several times to drive the post home. Its main advantage is that it does not split the top of the post, which can easily happen with a misdirected sledge hammer.

14. A natural ditch or depression in the ground makes a useful fence. Fix a pole and ground-line as shown in the drawing and the obstacle can be jumped from either direction.

15. A barbed wire fence close to an obstacle may cause concern if it is unprotected. We used old hosepipe, slit along its length and wrapped round the wire. This makes the wire easy to see and protects rider and pony from the barbs.

PUZZLE PAGE
ADDING UP

The answer to each of the following questions is a number. If you add all the answers together, the total has a particular significance for the Pony Club. Can you discover what it is?

1. How many parts to an in-and-out?
2. At what age do Pony Club members become associates?
3. How many faults for a knock-down at show jumping?
4. If my friend and I visit 19 horses, how many legs would there be?
5. How many native pony breeds in the British Isles?
6. How many tales of the Arabian Nights?
7. The trot is a pace of what time?
8. How many faults for taking an 'L' fence in the Cross Country phase of a one-day event?
9. What is the average normal Fahrenheit temperature of a horse?
10. How many took part in the Charge of the Light Brigade?
11. How many inches in a hand?
12. How many ribs has a horse?
13. What is the maximum height in inches of a Shetland pony?
14. At what age is a racehorse eligible to run in the Derby?
15. How many areas in the Pony Club?

Check your answers on page 60

53

The Reapers

by Caroline Strickland
illustrated by Ray Hutchins

The first drops of the rain that could rot our corn were falling, but the cart was wedged across the lane, blocking the other wagons. For all that the Shires strove, the heavy, backward drag of the cart would not let them gain a foothold . . .

I was fourteen the year we almost lost the corn. The harvest was late that summer; the spring had been so tardy that we thought the seed would never grow, but at last the young blades had shown, the fields had taken a bloom like the sheen on a cob and the wheat had hung ripe and heavy for the blade.

All this was over sixty years ago. We lived on a Yorkshire farm, running sheep on the heights and cultivating the small, stony meadows that lapped at the moor. My father had no trust in tractors and although our neighbours were changing to them our own work was done by horses – Dales to carry us, and strong, patient Shires to plough and cart.

The Dales were my own special care. The islanders of Scotland whose crofts were too small to need a heavy horse still shared my family's views and every season my mother and I bred and sold a handful of ponies to go to the cold, bleak lands of the Hebrides. It was a prejudice in those days that women could not raise good workers – old nagsmen would shake their heads and say we made the foals 'too gentle' but gentleness is no fault in animal or rider and our Dales were trained in the tradition of sires who had carried lead from the Northumberland mines to the sea, twenty or more docile, honest ponies winding through the drove roads controlled by only a single driver.

During harvest I would strap wicker panniers to Bess, our most placid mare, and ride up to the corn fields, squashed between the baskets laden with bread and cheese and oatmeal water, my legs clinging unorthodoxly to her shoulders, knowing that when I slid down to unload the food and take my place among the workmen I could trust her to make her way slowly back to the yard alone.

The sky that morning was sullen and the afternoon was one of heavy, troublesome heat. We were reaping the last acres of grain and I remember the rhythmic chunk of the binder as it cut its five-foot swathe through the rustling stalks. I was leading the wagon that would carry the sheaves down to the stack-yard to wait for threshing, and in other fields I could see my two brothers loading carts with stooked corn.

All that week had been dry and fine but this day was sultry and the threat of thunder meant we could not risk letting the crop lie in the fields. I fastened leafy twigs of elder into the brow-bands of Diamond and Whitefoot, lifting their rough forelocks to one side, brushing the gathering flies from the flat plates of their cheeks.

Whitefoot leaned back on his heels and shook himself like a dog emerging from a stream, jangling the harness of both and making the load sway and creak. I let them lower their muzzles to the ground and browse through the stubble as I forked the sheaves up on to the yellow mound that was rising in the cart, relying on them to answer to my voice when we needed to move further.

By the time the field was cleared and Tom, our farm-man, had packed the last of the wheat into place, a cool, moist breeze was blowing, bringing the astringent scent of the moor into the sweltering air of the harvest. I put my hand on Diamond's breeching and rested for a moment, looking back at what we had done.

"Feels like rain, Tom," I said, as he slid down from the stack and tightened the ropes that bound it to the cart.

"Aye," he strained at the last knot, "best be getting on," and then I knew that a storm was coming; Tom never used words when he thought that silence would do.

I heard a voice calling me and turned to see my father gesturing to us to carry our load down to the yard. Behind him my brothers' carts, piled high like shaggy, golden hillocks, were lumbering down the slope and, since the only entrance to the lane was through my field and there was little room to pass, I reached to take Diamond's rein – the leather wet and soapy from her sweat.

At the other side the bit chinked as Tom gathered Whitefoot and we urged them forward. They leaned into their collars, their smooth, black hair pressing hard against the checked cloth of the lining, and we moved off, the wheels crushing the straw under the great weight of the corn.

It was an awkward exit – a narrow opening, barely wide enough to take two horses, bounded by heavy stone gate-posts and forcing a sharp left-hand turn on to the track. There were great clouds building in the sky as we manoeuvred out of the field and the wind was fluttering stray stalks of wheat. The hub of a wheel grated against the wall but it did not catch and we were through and into the lane.

"Good girl, good girl," I said to Diamond and turned to check that the gate had not swung shut, but as I did so there was a dry, scraping slither, a frightened scuffling stamp of hooves, and the deep ruts of the parched lane crumbled under the pressure of the load, plunging the far wheel into the ditch.

The corn rocked and toppled. I leaped to unfasten the horses but, in an instant, as soon as it had begun, the confusion was over and all was still and quiet except for the dust that was being carried on the breeze and the snorting alarm of the Shires.

"Tom!" I called, afraid he had been thrown between the cart and wall, but he had jumped clear and was standing, hands on hips, beside me as my father and brothers came panting up to us.

I didn't know what to say. The cart was wedged across the lane, blocking the passage of other wagons, and the first light drops of rain that could rot our corn were falling. We were not large grain-growers and the three loads made the whole of our crop. Those were the years when a single loss could be a farmer's downfall and we had no coverings big enough to protect our wheat.

I felt Dad's fingers on my shoulder. "No fault of yours, lass," he said. "We'll take the gate off its hinges and fit it under the wheel. You bring the cart up over it."

We tried. Shires are slow but strong, willing workers and I stood at Diamond's head soothing and encouraging them, but for all that they strove, their muscles bunching with their effort, the heavy backward drag of the cart would not let them gain a foothold. The rain was spattering now, making round indentations in the dust and our clothes were clinging to us damply. The horses waiting with the other carts were becoming restless and I glanced at them as I heard them stir.

"Look!" I cried. "Single horses could pass. We could couple them in front."

The men ran to the wagons, undoing the gear of the two bays, their hands fumbling with haste. My father led Duchess to the gap between the protruding corner of the cart and the wall; she jibbed when she saw what she had to pass through but the pull on her rein was insistent. She pushed her 17 hands into

the narrow opening, her collar jarred the wagon, tilting it dangerously, and the boys clutched at its sides, hugging the wooden rails like drowning men, desperately using their weight to keep its wheels on the ground.

Duchess threw up her head, drawing in her hind legs as if she would rear but instead, finding herself so confined, she backed to the length of her rein, forcing her quarters into the face of Captain, who had been led behind her. He squealed – she bounded forward like a

great, startled cat and suddenly she was safely on to the track.

Captain followed, larger but more agile, and we buckled them frantically into a makeshift harness, lengthening their own traces with ropes tied to their hames.

My father and youngest brother took the leaders, Tom and I the wheelers, and, as the sky darkened overhead, casting a livid glow on us all, we gave the command. The cart shuddered as the Shires drew on their strength and slowly, painfully, it inched back on to solid ground.

We did not stop to look for damage. Racing now against the weather we bumped our first load down to the threshing-barn with the second rumbling in behind us and ran back, the bays outdistancing us with their deep, high-stepping trot, to drag the third. And, as we entered the farm-yard, relieved and exulting that all was gathered in, the lightning cracked and the thunder broke across the sky.

Ray Hutchins '82

ANGUS

by Jeanine Griffin, aged 9,
Burnley, Lancashire.

I have a pony,
He's ever so lowly.
He lives in a field
And eats all he can wield.
Ho goes inside in the winter
Comes out in the spring
To nosh and to nibble
The grass once again.

We went to a show and we won the first prize
And that was because my pony was wise.
If you searched the world over
And looked for a sign
Not one would you find
That was wiser than mine.

New Look at Old Sayings

by Lynda Stewart, Whitehead, Co. Antrim, Northern Ireland.

Too many oats spoil the broth.

Eat hay while the sun shines.

Pony today gone tomorrow.

A swish in time saves nine.

Sea Horses

by Lesley Zachary, aged 12,
Kanata, Ontario, Canada.

They sail across the wild waves,
Along the crested sea,
To greet the ocean's wondrous slaves,
That is, you and me.
They float along our midnight dreams
And kiss us in our sleep,
With the white foam as their bodies
And the wind as their seams.
Oh, come, you clear and clean horses,
Come, visit my dreams.
Come along your salty courses,
Amidst your glowing beams.

Horse's Head

by Dianne Malcolm, aged 16,
Elie, Fife, Scotland.

My Foal

by Jayne Taylor, aged 10,
Bransholme, Hull.

My foal is so gentle,
So kind and so good.
He treats me like a princess,
Like every horse should.

But my foal is special,
He's just like a dog,
So playful, so silky,
But he's a bit of a hog.

I think of my foal, by night and by day,
And I say to my mam, don't ever take him away.
I love my foal and there's nothing else to say!

My Friend

by Debra Fettes, aged 14,
Tradespark, Nairn-shire.

Wild eyed, full of spirit
Thundering across the field,
Ploughing up the hard earth in his stride;
The ferocious wind being left behind.

Alone and desolate he often stands,
Stretching to his utmost height in hands.
No one seems to care for him;
Although when passing they stop and stare,
Some with hatred in their eyes:
Others amazed and very surprised.

He's sweet and loving in every way.
How can people be so cruel?
To treat this creature like a fool.
There's only one thing left to say
That we are friends and friends we'll stay.

The Derby

by Joanne Lawson, aged 12,
Newton Hall, Durham.

The excitement rises,
There's a crash in the stalls,
Another Derby's started,
The Epsom crowd calls.

The horses are galloping,
They get faster all the time.
The favourite is leading,
The bookies think it's a crime.

The crowd rises,
A furlong to go.
From the stands, there is shouting,
Go, horses, go.

Who is going to win?
We will soon find out.
The bay passes the finish,
He's won without a doubt.

He was a Beauty

by Kerry Homer, aged 13,
Pensnett, Brierley Hill,
West Midlands.

I had a jet black horse,
He was beautiful of course,
His eyes would shine so bright
With glee or sometimes fright.

I groomed him every day
In my own careful way,
And when he went to sleep
A-standing he would keep.

He was so alert and fearful.
And in his duties cheerful
When we went out for a ride,
He joggled my insides.

My First Cross-Country Event

By Caroline Potts, aged 8,
Fogo, Duns, Berwickshire.

Just finished his round, number 23,
Next to go, oh, help, it's me.
Up to the start and off we go,
Reach the first fence, thank goodness it's low.
Safely over, my pony jumps well,
Will I clear the rest? Only she can tell.
She carries me on, over ditches and rails,
And pops out neatly over the bales.
Steady now, down quite a steep hill,
We'll clear the water, I know we will.
Over the brush, the barrels too,
Clear so far, only one to do.
As we approach, my heart's beating fast,
Can she do it, jump clear at the last?
Safely over, the spectators cheer,
"Well done, lass," I shout in her ear.
The excitement at finishing is not over yet,
When the results come out, Vanity wins a
            ROSETTE!

DREAMS

by Sarah Cartwright, aged 12,
Walmley, Sutton Coldfield,
West Midlands.

If I could have a pony,
Which one would I choose?
Which colour, breed, what age?
Would he have shining shoes?
Or would he have bare hooves
Which galloped on the moor?
A Dartmoor with his four stout legs
Which stand so squarely on the floor.
An Arab which jumped like a dream,
A stocky Shetland, small but keen.
Or perhaps a Welsh with a
A thorough

HORSE'S HEAD
CROSSWORD

WORD SEARCH

ADDING UP

1.	2	8.	10
2.	17	9.	100
3.	4	10.	600
4.	80	11.	4
5.	9	12.	36
6.	1001	13.	42
7.	2	14.	3
		15.	19

1929   This was the date
when the Pony Club
was founded

JUNIOR SHOW JUMPER

Well, were you right? The young
boy jumping at Roehampton in
1947 is, of course, none other
than Ted Edgar.